Hey unbound one!

Welcome to this magical book brought to you by The Unbound Press.

At The Unbound Press we believe that when women write freely from the fullest expression of who they are, it can't help but activate a feeling of deep connection and transformation in others. When we come together, we become more and we're changing the world, one book at a time!

This book has been carefully crafted by both the author and publisher with the intention of inspiring you to move ever more deeply into who you truly are.

We hope that this book helps you to connect with your Unbound Self and that you feel called to pass it on to others who want to live a more fully expressed life.

With much love,

Nicola Hu

Founder of The Unbound Press

www.theunboundpress.com

CONTENTS

INITIATION
OF A
GODDESS

RECLAIM THE
MAGIC AND POWER
OF YOUR INNER GODDESS!

LISA MELBOURNE

The information given in this book should not be treated as a substitute for professional medical advice; always consult a medical practitioner. Any use of information in this book is at the reader's discretion and risk. Neither the author nor the publisher can be held responsible for any loss, claim or damage arising out of the use, or misuse, of the suggestions made, the failure to take medical advice or for any material on third party websites.

ISBN:
978-1-916529-29-8 (Paperback)
978-1-916529-30-4 (Ebook)

Cover design by Lynda Mangoro.

The Unbound Press
www.theunboundpress.com

ᴅEFINITION OF A GODDESS

1. A female being of supernatural powers or attributes, believed in and worshipped by a people.

2. A female being believed to be the source of life and worshipped as the principal deity in various religions.

3. An image of a female supernatural being; an idol.

4. Something, such as fame or wealth, that is worshipped or idealised.

5. A woman of great beauty or grace

– The Free Dictionary, by FARLEX 2020

Hello and welcome to *Initiation of a Goddess*. For those of you who know my work and have read my first book, *Natural Magic for the Modern Goddess*, you will know that I am dedicated to helping women create a life of self and spiritual empowerment, fully committed to who they are and what they want from life.

By connecting and synchronising our body and our energies with the natural world, the moon, seasons and natural healing, we not only reconnect our body and soul to our earthly home, but we also re-discover our way back home to who we are with a deeper love and commitment to living a life of meaning, passion, creativity, connectivity and purpose.

What does it mean to be a Goddess? The definitions that you will find will all point towards the perception and belief that others have of a Goddess and yet, there is no mention of how a Goddess perceives herself to be the Goddess that she is, that we all are.

My hope for this book is that it will not only remind you, dear reader, that you are, have been and will always be a uniquely divine Goddess within the eyes of the Universe but also guide and support you in fully committing to the worship of yourself, first and foremost. This will open your eyes, your heart, and your soul, and you will be able to witness that you are in fact the Goddess that you have been waiting for all along, and maybe you just didn't recognise her until now.

We will focus on how and what it means to connect with our Inner Goddess throughout this book, but first, let's think about what it might mean to initiate ourselves into the ways of the Goddess. Where are we starting as we begin this journey? Well, the word *start* is a very good place to start. An initiation is a right of passage, the beginning of something new and often something deeply transforming. The word *initiation* is often associated with secrecy and private societies that request their members perform rites and take part in secret rituals before being officially recognised as members of the society. An initiation is a deeply personal experience that we will carry with us for lifetimes, and that is where we find ourselves as we dive between the pages of this book.

You are about to take a leap into a new chapter in life, creating your own sacred rituals that will guide you along the way to re-discovering your Inner Goddess and beginning a conscious journey with a deeper connection to yourself than you have ever had before.

To fully acknowledge your Inner Goddess, seeing her for the magical, unique part of you that has always been there, you must learn to dive deep into the very heart of who you are. You must embrace every single part of you – mind, body and spirit – learning to love yourself with a deepness as vast and as rich as the ocean.

Do you want loving and positive relationships with others? You must nurture a loving and positive relationship with yourself first. When you radiate love, a deep and unconditional love for yourself, then your energy becomes magnetic, reaching out to others in an energetic and subconscious way that you are a person who is loved so very much and is deserving and accepting of love from another.

Are you in a relationship that makes you feel less than, inadequate, with your own wants and needs at the bottom of the pile? It will be hard to admit but if you turn the focus inwards towards your relationship with yourself, you will find that the reason that you attract unfulfilling relationships is because you have an unfulfilling relationship with yourself. You will view yourself as less important so you will invest very little time in yourself and your own self-care. You will take those deep breaths each day and move through the heaviness of life because you will feel undeserving of the contentment that comes with a deeply profound inner happiness at your core.

On a conscious level, you may not even realise that you have been viewing yourself this way for as long as you can remember. This is just part of your outlook on life, on you, who and how you are at a cellular level. You accept that how you view yourself is normal, that it would perhaps be egotistical to think any higher of yourself. For, who are you to think that you are beautiful, funny, talented, and exceptional by simply being *you*?

Well, I am here to remind you of just how incredibly worthy you are of everything you have ever dreamt of and more, and most of all, how worthy you are of being you.

To own your Inner Goddess is to fully own yourself, to be able to consciously envelop every single part of you in a rich layer of love and appreciation for everything that you are.

To live a life as a Goddess is to ever-evolve, adapt and be mindful of creating space for your evolution. Always flow, encourage, question and dig deeper into your soul to seek out the truth of who you are and what you came here to share with the world.

To be a Goddess is to be perfectly imperfect and to adore every part of you.

To be a Goddess is to love and cherish your body, to treat her like your loving best friend.

To think like a Goddess is to follow your intuition whether it makes sense or not. Trusting that you don't always have to know the answers.

To be a Goddess is to view every situation from a place of love, trust and positivity, knowing that, despite how difficult things might be right now, something incredible is on its way.

To be a Goddess is to have a deep connection to nature, the moon and the cosmos for they will shine a light on your own nature that mirrors the cyclical magic of the natural world and the cosmos.

After the storm, there is always sunshine.

This book will take you on a journey of self-discovery, diving deeper than you have ever gone before in order to reconnect with the Goddess that resides within us all, so that you might find love, compassion and adoration for the exquisite being that you are. So that you might live a life fully enriched in the knowledge that you are worthy of being you and therefore, worthy of everything that you have ever wished for.

Your first tick in the box is for choosing this book, for perhaps not fully understanding why you chose it, but for choosing it anyway because something in your heart called for you to connect with it. That 'something' was your Inner Goddess whispering, nudging you to connect with her fully and wholly because it is time. It is time to do the work and dig deep into the richness of your soul. It is time to start creating a life you love full of passion, love, creativity and connectedness and it all starts with you.

Welcome, Goddess.

You have arrived!

FIVE PILLARS OF GODDESS

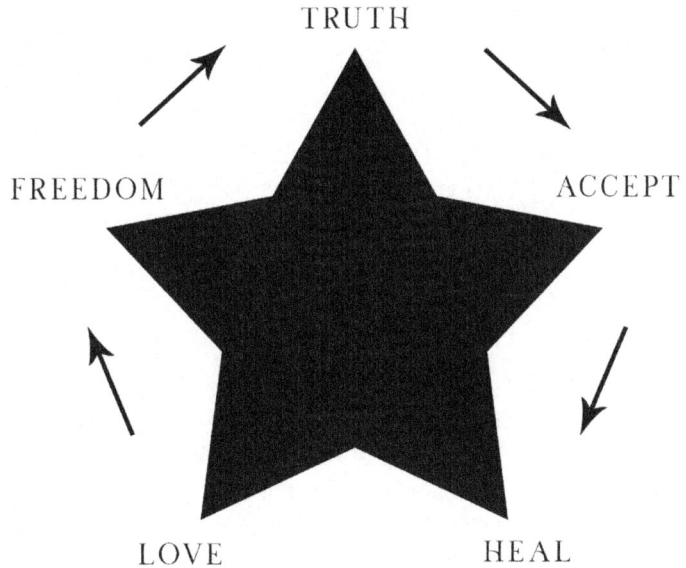

TRUTH

FREEDOM

ACCEPT

LOVE

HEAL

TRUTH – To witness and honour the truth of who you are.

ACCEPT – To accept all that has been and gone and is present.

HEAL – To honour past truths, stories and pain, and the wisdom and strength they have given you.

LOVE – To love yourself in the light and the darkness. Unconditionally.

FREEDOM – To move out of your own way and let your Goddess choose her own unique path through life.

This book is comprised of five parts, each representing one of the Five Pillars of Goddess. It is through my experience of working with women and supporting them to heal their mind, body, soul and sense of spirit over the past 12 years that I have come to realise that we must heal, nurture and honour each of these five parts of ourselves so that we may find healing, inner peace, a sense of equilibrium within our physical, mental and spiritual health, acceptance for what has been and what now is, and ultimately, the freedom to live our life, happy within our own skin and in the way that we choose.

Within each section flows part of my own story with the hope that if my own experiences resonate with you, you may find comfort in knowing that you are not alone while also finding clarity in your way forward with the support of mindful tools, rituals, meditations and journaling prompts.

PILLAR ONE

TRUTH

To understand the truth of who you are, you must first find acceptance for who you are and where you find yourself to be in life. So often we wonder how we have ended up with the stories and experiences that have led us to this point in life, wondering if we could have done things differently, made different choices, been someone else. But the truth is, there was never meant to be any other way for you. If there was, then so it would be.

When you find acceptance for what is and how things have unfolded for you in your life, you will begin to take more of a conscious role in how you want your life to unfold and pan out. You will be able to step back and gain some perspective on the choices that you make and why you make them. You will actively take more control of your life rather than feeling like you are being carried along by an invisible source that keeps throwing things in your way that you didn't ask for and don't make you happy.

When you really dive into the in-between spaces between major decisions that you have made and where the motivation behind those decisions comes from, you will start to understand not only what drives you but also what triggers you into making those decisions. You will notice recurring patterns within the stories of your life that may or may not hold some regret for you with the wish that things could have been different.

Understanding the truth of who you are means that you accept all of you, you accept the parts of you that you wish were different and you accept and honour the desires that you have within your heart to give yourself what will nourish you, make you happy and fulfil your needs.

A JOURNEY HOME

For those of you who have not met me before, my name is Lisa and you might say that it took me just over three decades to truly make contact with my Inner Goddess.

I grew up in a very masculine world with heavy masculine influences. My dad was an Army Officer and my brother a Royal Marine. I went to a military boarding school and I come from a long line of military ancestors. It really was inevitable that I would go on to join the military myself, having spent the first few years of my adult life working as a civil servant with the Navy before joining the RAF as a medic.

The driving force behind every decision in my life was to connect with the masculine, whether it was through my choice of career, my relationship with my dad, or the choice of life partner that I made. The masculine influence was strong and most important to me.

There was a major imbalance of the feminine and masculine, and it didn't come to light until I left the military and became a mother – straight out of the masculine fire and into the watery depths of the feminine.

For the first time in my life, I was faced with my emotions and no way of escaping from them. I had no way of ignoring them or burying them underneath work. Instead I was confronted with an overwhelming barrage of deep, inner turmoil that I had no choice but to confront and work my way through in order to find my way back to myself.

The trouble is, when life becomes decidedly less busy, it is only then that the internal noise and chatter rises to the surface, becoming so deafening that it is hard to ignore.

I had spent the previous six years moving forward at a fast pace, experiencing the new and the unusual/extreme on a daily basis, so much so that living a life out of my comfort zone had in fact become my comfort zone. But here it was that I had found myself all of a sudden, thrown in at the deep end of all that was normal and every-day, and it felt completely foreign to me.

I discovered in my late teens that to be able to feel contentment and at peace in my life, I was the kind of person who needed to have a clearly defined purpose. If I didn't have a purpose I would start to flounder, and so it was that I always kept myself and my life moving forward.

Looking back, I can still feel the deep unsettled feeling that I believe I was always aware of, but instead of facing it and understanding it, I ran from it. I felt like I always had something to prove to someone else when in fact, the person I was trying to prove myself to was me.

Having never had a real place on this planet to call home because we always moved with Dad's job, I think the feeling was one of deep un-rootedness to life and the people around me. I had no anchor to hold me in place, and for a long time I believed that it was because I had no real physical connection to a little corner of this planet that I could call home.

It wasn't until my soul cracked open at the age of 28 when I realised it was myself whom I had never felt at home with. I discovered a complete disconnection to myself on every level. I didn't understand myself, or care or pay much attention to my thoughts and my feelings. The only time that I did was when I berated myself for how I looked, either too podgy, too dumpy, too stocky, too spotty ... the list was endless of my major disappointments that I held myself accountable to on a daily basis.

I realised for the first time in my life that I really didn't care a great deal about myself, and yet I spent the majority of my life wanting other people to love and care for me as a validation of my worthiness, of being deserving in some way of being here in this life, as me on this planet.

I was looking for love – the ultimate feeling of home that was evading me. It took me a long time to realise, however, that I, me, myself, am in fact already home.

Ask yourself, what does *home* feel like to you? For me, it is a place of familiarity, a place that I know inside out, somewhere that I feel safe, secure and happy. A place full of comforting memories and trinkets that remind me of who I am and where I have been. A home is filled with the things we love to be around. We enjoy treating our home to gifts, makeovers and facelifts in order to enhance the love that we have for our home and how much we love to spend time in it.

Our home is our cave, a place that is sacred and nourishing to our soul. Where would we be without it?

This is how we should be caring and loving ourselves.

Now I'm not saying that it isn't important to have a home and a nice one at that, but sometimes when we find ourselves focusing outside of ourselves for a feeling or a part of our life that is missing, we should in fact be turning inwards and exploring where that feeling, or belief is coming from within ourselves.

You can create the most beautiful home in the world, but if you are struggling to find a feeling of contentment in your life, feeling unfulfilled, lonely, adrift or directionless, a nice home filled with things won't take those feelings away.

The answers always lie within us and how at home we feel within our own skin.

Think of yourself as you would your home. If you stop loving it, cleaning it, maintaining it, it will become dilapidated, it will lose its vibrant energy that makes you and others feel happy, warm and welcome. Things will stop working properly and the cobwebs will clog up the lovely clean air. You will not want to spend time in it because it won't make you feel good.

Your body and how you feel and treat it will respond in the same way.

Your health might deteriorate, your energy levels reduce, your self-confidence shrink and the feeling of being unloved and adrift will grow because you show yourself no love and affection and haven't spent the time nurturing and honouring the physical home to your soul, therefore feeling disconnected and homeless.

When I realised that the answer to every problem that I'd ever had, every emotion that I had ever struggled with, every negative perspective I had ever endured could be found at the root of who I was, the blinkers came off. The light came on and I could see the piece of the puzzle that had evaded me for most of my life so clearly.

I needed to reconnect to myself, get to really know, love and nurture every part of myself, hold space for myself, listen to myself, appreciate and spend time with myself. I needed to dig so deep and start back at the very beginning of all that I knew about me in order to ignite a spark of deep transformation and change.

It has been eleven years since I discovered that I was the home that I had been looking for all along, and in that time I have dedicated and committed myself not only to being my own biggest and most loyal fan but also to creating a fresh start and a life that flows in synchronicity with who I am continually becoming.

When you discover who you are, allowing the Goddess within you to have a voice and be heard above all else, life will start to fall into place, and it will start to flow more effortlessly. You will embrace the struggles from a deeper place of learning, appreciating the lessons that you will learn from them. You will live a life all-in and with no regrets. You will attract much deeper, meaningful and more aligned relationships, you will experience a deeper fulfilment and purpose than you ever did before.

Life will feel good and you will own it.

Soul Question

Do you feel at home within yourself? Explain your answer.

GODDESS INITIATION

Make a pledge to yourself on the night of the next New Moon that you will fully immerse yourself from this day forward into following the call of your Inner Goddess. The New Moon is also known as the Dark Moon, when the moon cannot be seen in our night sky because it is fully immersed in the shadow of Earth.

New Moons are a time for introspection and new beginnings, the perfect time for mindfully committing to new projects and goals. The initiatory energy of the New Moon will add a dash of magic to your mindful practices helping to carry them forward to fruition.

To find out which current phase the moon is in, you can google it – or why not treat yourself to one of the many beautiful moon journals out there on the market?

TAKE A CLEANSING ROSE BATH

On the night of the New Moon, cook yourself some healthy, nourishing food and commit fully to an evening of self-care – time spent just on you.

Afterwards, run yourself a bath and add your favourite colour rose petals to the water. Make sure you save a few for after your bath too. The rose symbolises love and embodies the Divine Feminine energy that flows throughout our veins.

Add 4-7 drops of pure rose essential oil to 10mls/1 tbsp of carrier oil such as sweet almond or sunflower and add to the bath before swishing to disperse. Rose essential oil has a balancing effect on the female reproductive system, connecting us on a much deeper level to our femininity and Inner Goddess.

Climb into your luxurious bath and spend some time relaxing your mind and your body. Allow the soft energies of the rose to surround you as you relax and let go of any tension.

Focus on relaxing the whole of your body, starting at the top of your head and working your way down like a relaxation scanner, loosening up any tense or tight areas as you scan your thoughts over your body.

Breathe in for four seconds through your nose, and out for four seconds through your mouth.

Relax and breathe.

The healing properties of the rose essential oil will be softly filtering into your body and circulating to the places where it is needed most.

Imagine soft pink energy from the rose oil filling you with a deep sense of calm and appreciation for all that your body does to support you every single day.

Take note of any areas of discomfort or tightness. If you are struggling with tension in your upper back, shoulders and neck, you might be feeling a little overwhelmed with responsibilities right now. You may feel the burden of others relying on you but lack a support network yourself. Reach out. The chances are you are not alone, it is just perhaps that you are too proud to ask for help.

If you suffer with lower back problems it may be that you are worrying about money and finances, and again, feel unsupported and weighed down with taking on the worry of it all.

Hips, knees and ankles are related on a metaphysical level to feeling that you are stuck or trapped in your circumstances. You are unhappy and unsure of how or if you can move forward. There is a certain level of guilt that is eating away at you because of how you feel.

For a more in-depth look at the mind/body connection, check out my first book-baby, *Natural Magic for the Modern Goddess*.

Allow yourself a minimum of 15-20 minutes to enjoy your Goddess Initiation Bath before climbing out and dressing in something soft and comfortable.

Once dressed, find somewhere that you won't be disturbed and bring with you two pieces of paper and a pen, your favourite candle and crystal. Place them in your sacred space before preparing yourself a cleansing and detoxifying herbal tea.

You will need:

- Cinnamon sticks – a diuretic and full of antioxidants
- Cardamom pods
- Ginger

Boil a pan of water and add the ingredients.

Simmer for ten minutes, strain and serve.

Take your tea back to your sacred space along with a small dish, some carrier oil and your rose essential oil. If you are able to find a spot near a window or even outside so that you can look up at the sky, that would be wonderful, but not essential.

Light your candle and add 5-10mls of your carrier oil to your dish. Add two drops of rose to the oil and swish the dish to blend the oils.

Dip your forefinger and middle finger into the oil and apply as a dab to the space just above the centre of your eyebrows.

Now dab your fingers onto your chest above your heart space, just once.

Scatter the remaining rose petals in a circle around you and your candle, crystal, pen and paper. This space is now sealed and sacred.

Take a moment to ground your energy by imagining thick roots growing from the soles of your feet, down deep into Mother Earth. Feel held and supported by her as you centre your thoughts and clear your mind.

Relax your shoulders and focus on your breathing for a couple of minutes – in through your nose for four seconds and out through your mouth for four seconds.

Look up at the sky and imagine that with every inhale, you breathe in the light and the energy of the Universe, the stars, the planets, the invisible moon and all of creation.

Breathe in new beginnings, new life with a deeper connection to who you are and where you come from – you are part of the rich vastness of the Universe.

With your left hand over your heart, pick up your crystal and hold it in the palm of your right hand. Repeat the following words, feeling them seep into every cell and fibre of your being.

Universe, hear me this night,
As I (your name here)
Pledge this oath to you and the Goddess
Within me.
This is my initiation.
This is my new beginning.
This is my unravelling.
This is my story.
This is my light, and I am ready
To stand fully within it.
I am cracking open,
Releasing old wounds,
Unleashing my wild soul
And remembering my ancient wisdom.
I stand here for me,
I stand here for the women that came
Before me,
And I stand here
For the women that will come
After.
I vow to honour the lessons
In all things, good and bad,
Light and dark,
Hard and easy.
I vow to always listen

To the whispers of the Goddess
Within,
Honour the light that she shines bright
And love my self wholly
And unconditionally,
Because I am love,
With every breath,
I see it, feel it, touch it, invoke it.
I will always feel worthy
And cherish my mind, body and soul
For the Goddess I am.
I will always be good enough,
Brave enough, strong enough,
To follow the calling of my soul,
Wherever the Goddess leads me.
For I am She
And She is me.
I am the Earth, Moon, Stars and Ether.
I am everything
And everything is me.
This is my sacred oath,
My sacred initiation of
The Goddess.
And so it is!

Close your eyes and just take a moment to really lean into the vibrant energy that is currently swirling all around you, within and without.

Know that you have set into motion something truly epic. You have re-opened the sacred door within and embraced your Inner Goddess.

From this moment on, trust that wherever you go you are on the right path and that everything that unfolds is for your highest good.

Keep your crystal close to you always, to remind you of the oath you made to yourself. This crystal is connected to you, now and forever, infused with the magic and the call of your Inner Goddess. Let it be a reminder of the inner strength, love and wisdom that you possess whenever you are filled with worry and self-doubt.

Take soothing and cleansing sips of your tea as you journal on the following questions. Write the first six questions on one piece of paper and the other seven on the second piece.

1. **How did I feel about myself before my Goddess Initiation?**

2. **What emotions, energy and situations do I not want to bring with me into this new chapter of my life?**

3. **Do my life and current circumstances fulfil me and make me happy?**

4. **What, if anything, would I like to change about my life and why?**

5. **Why have I felt unable to change my current circumstances?**

6. What led to me realising that I have disconnected from my Inner Goddess?

7. List all the things I love about myself.

8. Write/create my very own positive affirmation to connect with daily that sums up my greatest desire for this new journey. For example:

   'I love myself unconditionally and always follow my intuition.'

9. What one small step can I take towards the change that I am craving daily?

10. Which way does my intuition serve me best? It could be a gut feeling, a sign/presence of a particular animal or insect, or divination with cards such as tarot or spirit downloads and messages planted within my dreams. Make a conscious effort to pay attention to your intuition every day.

11. How do I want to feel about myself and my life?

12. Is there something new I want to learn?

13. Do I connect with nature enough? If not, how can I connect with nature more?

Read through your answers again, honouring the voice of your Inner Goddess that is now being heard.

Burn the first piece of paper with the first six answers on it, feeling the weight of them and what has been, release its grip from you.

Keep the other page with 7-13 somewhere you can re-read them from time to time to help keep you focussed and motivated.

You can now finish your sacred initiation circle. You can leave the rose petals to be blown away if you are outside or you can gather them up and scatter them outside as an offering to the Universe and the moon.

You might want to keep a handful to use as potpourri. Just lay them to dry on your windowsill for a few days until they are crispy and add them to a cute little dish. You could sprinkle a few drops of your rose essential oil over them to enjoy their deeply nourishing scent throughout your living space too.

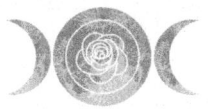

Your passion
is your mission

Your passion is your mission

Your life is your purpose

Your joy is your freedom

Your heart is your compass.

YOUR JOURNEY SO FAR

A very good place to start with is where you are at right now. If you know where you are, you can figure out where you are going.

So, where are you in your life right now? Something about where you are led you to me, to picking up this book and deciding that it was something you needed right now.

Did you happen to be travelling merrily along in life with your head down, focussed on getting through each day that, one day you looked up and realised that you had somehow arrived here, and that actually, it has been a bit of a bloody shock?

You ask yourself over and over, 'How on Earth did this happen? Where did the last ten years of my life go?'

Were you expecting to still be *here*, in this job, this town, this relationship? Or was there some long-forgotten part of you that once dreamt of being somewhere else, doing something else, with someone else?

There comes a point for most of us when life catches up and we realise that what we wanted when we first set out on this path has changed. It is no longer what we desire, and it no longer makes us happy, and I'm here to share with you that it's OK. In fact, it's perfectly normal for you to change and want different things out of life. No longer is it the 'norm' to stay in a job for life or a relationship for that matter.

Our society's expectations are changing all the time and with the age of technology has come a complete overhaul to our job spectrum. There is quite literally a job for everything and if there isn't, it doesn't take long before someone creates one.

More and more of us are deciding to create a life that is on our terms, doing something that ignites a passion and excitement within us rather than the dread of a lifelong career of misery as part of something that doesn't light us up or make us feel good.

People are waking up and realising that there is more to life than just getting by and paying the bills and doing what is seen to be the right thing.

We are so lucky to live in this incredible age of opportunity and connection. We literally have access to every corner of the planet, and if we use this gift in a wise, nurturing and mindful way, we can live the life of our dreams.

There is no one to tell us we can't, only ourselves.

We are usually the only one standing in our way. How long have you been standing in your own way? I bet, like me, you didn't even realise that you were doing it, did you?

So, where are you now?

Are you where you really want to be?

Do you love your job and feel passionately about it? Or do you struggle to get through the day, dislike the company, the people, or what your organisation stands for?

Do you view your job as a way of making a living, or do you see your job as a calling, a part of who you are that represents your passions and beliefs?

It is important to mention here of course that it is OK to not have a job that you are passionate about. A lot of us wouldn't know what that is anyway. For a lot of people, an element to finding contentment in life comes from having a solid and dependable job that allows them to live comfortably, enjoy nice holidays and have nice things.

Everyone's idea of the perfect life is different, and a lot of the mental health problems that we as a society face today come from people feeling that what they have is never enough, always wanting more or believing that they should have more when in a lot of cases, more of something does not equate to more happiness. More things, a bigger house, better holidays, flashy cars and a ton of money in the bank ... the list becomes endless and a lot of this is driven by our need to share and compare on social media.

We are starting to experience the very real mental health condition of FOMO ('Fear of Missing Out') within our society, and in particular our younger generations who feel that they should want, have, and need the same as everyone else in order to be recognised as successful and to fit within their peer groups.

I wonder whether, given the time to step back and take everybody else's opinion out of the equation, those who feel like they struggle with FOMO would recognise that they might not want all of those things in excess at all? If we were to take away consumerism, what would we be left with wanting out of life? I believe that it would in fact feel like a reset button for us all. We would re-focus our attentions on loving and cherishing the relationships we have, appreciate the satisfaction we get from working and providing for ourselves, and seek adventure, wonder, excitement and contentment in places still unknown to us on this planet.

Why aren't these things seen as enough anymore?

Some of the most content people that I have met are not those that have thousands in the bank with the big expensive car and humungous home, they are in fact the people who have the perfect (or damn close) work/life balance where they can leave work at the door and enjoy time with loved ones and moments of introspection. Being able to quite literally stop and smell the roses. They can do this because they have created enough time to be fully present and enjoy the seemingly little things that are so often missed because we are too busy chasing the next thing.

It is also important to note that if you are driven to live a life full of the finer things with opportunities to indulge in regular luxury, with a career that pays handsomely and rewards you well, then that is ok too. So many people find themselves stuck financially, secretly wishing they could earn more because they deserve more, but dismiss it because they think that wanting more makes them greedy and selfish and that everyone else would think they are greedy and selfish too.

We are all entitled to have our dreams and aspirations that are as unique and as different as we are. We shouldn't be judged for wanting more or less than anyone else.

So, are you a person who has a dependable job with a dependable income? Or, do you have a job that defines who you are and what you are passionate about?

Are you happy with your job? Or do you feel that it no longer fits who you are or what you want?

Do you long to be in the other category?

Spend time journaling around these questions. If you are seeking change, ask yourself which category that change would fall into.

A tip to figuring out what your true calling may be is to think about any hobbies that you have or perhaps had as a child.

What do you love to read about? Watch or talk about with friends? Often these things are overlooked for what they really are. Why can't you make a living out of a hobby? Someone else has so why can't you?

Whichever conclusion you come to, avoid the overwhelm and break the next steps down into lots of little manageable steps. Focus on each little step rather than the entire journey.

Let's now take a look at your personal life. You might think that this is awfully nosey of me, but I promise you that a lot of clues can be found within our relationships that correlate with the way we really feel about ourselves.

Are you in a relationship? A happy one? Or do you perhaps long for a relationship with the right person and yet, you somehow always end up with Mr/Mrs Wrong?

Are you scared to have a relationship?

Or perhaps you don't want one at all? You are perfectly happy on your own?

Our relationships and the kind of relationships that we attract are a mirror of ourselves. It is my belief that we are not all necessarily made to have one forever perfect love in our life. Some people do of course, but I believe we are often made to feel that we should all have that one true love because of society's expectations.

Long-term relationship or not, I believe that what works for one doesn't have to work for another. We shouldn't feel defined by our relationships or fit our relationships into what the world thinks they should be. Each and every one of us is different and unique with different wants and needs in this lifetime. Wherever you may find yourself right now, take some time to step back and view your relationships (friendships and working relationships included) as an observer. What do you see and notice about these relationships and the impact they have on you when you adjust your perspective?

SOUL QUESTIONS

Do your relationships make you feel good? Explain

Think back to the beginning of an important relationship in your life. How different was your relationship at the beginning compared to how it makes you feel now? How has it evolved? How does the person make you feel now compared to back then?

Do you feel that you can meet a new common ground with this person? If so, what would it be?

Is it time to let go of a relationship that no longer make you happy?

Remember, it's natural for things to come to an end in order to make way for something new and more aligned with who you are now.

ℒET'S START WITH YOU

Let's think back to the New Moon Initiation and some of the answers that you wrote down to the guided questions. You are now at the very start of your Goddess Path and a large part of the journey will be paved regularly with time out to do the really deep inner work. By this, I mean re-addressing the demons in your closet that may not have been dealt with properly. Really getting to the core of where you are at right now, in the present and always realigning yourself with your path as it twists and turns.

We are always evolving and growing and changing our goals, and so it is important to take the time to ask ourselves, '*How does this current situation make me feel? Am I happy? Do I feel fulfilled? How do I feel about myself right now?*'

Vigilance with our thoughts is key because our thoughts create habits that can be hard to break. Those sly little digs and negative comments we tell ourselves will slip back in on a daily basis under the radar if we aren't careful.

Take a moment to think about your day so far. When you were standing in front of the mirror this morning, putting your makeup on or brushing your teeth, what thoughts passed through your mind? Is the first thing that you usually tell yourself something along the lines of, '*Ugh, you look tired/spotty/old/ugly today*'?

What about when you were choosing what to wear? Did you make the conscious decision not to wear something because of how bad it made you feel? What were your thoughts when you looked in the mirror? Were your eyes drawn, as always, to your tummy, expecting it to look flabby and noticeable, for example?

The same goes for when you made yourself breakfast this morning, or how much you might have berated yourself for not having more patience with the kids when you were trying to get them ready for school and they just wouldn't put their shoes on!

These little moments throughout your day create an enormous picture of your general vibe that passes like an undercurrent, a continuous stream of unheard noise through your mind, body and spirit that has now become the norm due to its constant presence.

It is time to learn to tune in again to this undercurrent, stopping it in its tracks and replacing negative thoughts and comments with something positive and loving instead. It will take you a while to start believing the words that you are telling yourself, for the compliments to be accepted and cherished, taken straight into the heart, but it will happen. You just need to override the system and this will take some time, so be patient with yourself.

Tell yourself that you are doing your best, even if you don't believe it. Tell yourself that you are beautiful, even if you don't feel it. Thank your body for waking up with you every single morning, for carrying you through the day and supporting you.

Someone, somewhere in the world won't wake up today. They might take their last breath today, or perhaps lose the function of their body today. I bet you'd be desperate to keep your body just the way it is if today might be the last day before it is taken away from you.

Let's now dig a little deeper into the relationship that you have with yourself. You may want to grab a pen and journal to write your answers down for these questions. Try to explain your answer rather than leaving it as a yes or no.

How do you feel about your body?

How do you feel about yourself as a person, do you love who you are?

Are you grateful for being you?

Have you always struggled with positive self-perception?

Think back to when you were little and growing up. Most of us felt complete and utter freedom within our bodies as children. Loving the freedom of learning to move, crawl and walk. Feeling proud of our self and our body for learning to ride a bike or roller-skate, or run, or jump the highest. Our mind was free from the endless negative constraints that may now perhaps plague our daily thoughts and drag us down.

As children, we embraced our body's ability to learn and do new things all of the time. Not once did we worry that we might look ridiculous doing it. Living in our young body meant only that days were filled with adventure and learning new skills.

Allow your mind to carry you forward now to a time when you first remember your feelings for yourself starting to change, perhaps becoming more aware of how you felt and looked. For most of us, this usually happens around the time that puberty kicks in.

What was happening in your life back then?

Was your home life happy?

What was your relationship like with your parents?

Was your mother happy and content, or did she appear to struggle with her own happiness?

Did you feel settled at school with good friends or did you feel lonely and struggle to make friends?

Just take a few moments to sit quietly and visualise that younger version of you, whenever it might have been, imagining that you are standing facing her with arms wide open. Imagine her moving forward as you wrap your arms around her and tell her that everything is OK, that she is loved and that she is worthy of being loved.

Tell her that she is beautiful and that you are proud of her and who she is going to become.

Tell her that the only person who can make her happy is herself. If she loves herself for everything that she is, she will invite the most beautiful friendships and relationships into her life. She will find a deep, inner contentment that will stay with her for a lifetime.

Just take a moment more to stand there holding your younger self.

When I did this exercise myself for the first time, I remember the fierce rush of emotion that came flooding to the surface. Emotion that ran deep with a fierce, protective energy for the little girl that I was holding, but laced with a newfound awareness for the tremendous amount of hurt and pain that I had put myself through throughout my life.

I saw myself as the innocent girl I was and the light that shone so brightly within her, me, that I had slowly and repetitively tried to stamp out over the course of my lifetime.

I saw this little girl as *my* two little girls, stood before me. The thought of either one of them putting themselves through what I had put myself through was just too much to bear.

This was a pivotal moment for me in my initiation into reclaiming my Inner Goddess.

TASK

Write a letter to the child-you, telling her, reminding her of all the things that you love about her.

What advice would you give her knowing what you know now?

How would you help her to navigate the choppy waters of life ahead of her with self-love and care?

Once you have written it read it aloud and burn it on the night of a Full Moon with gratitude in your heart. Full moons are a time of gratitude and release. Themes of letting go are strong. The Full Moon will support you in letting go of the hurt and the guilt, replacing it with feelings of love and gratitude for the Goddess that you now acknowledge yourself to be.

Keep your inner child close to you to remind you to pay yourself and her a kindness every day.

CHANGE IS COMING

Change is coming,

It is alchemical and potent,

It is light and dark,

It reaches between the cracks of your soul,

Trying you on for size.

You sense it

Like the change in the air

When a new season approaches.

Something new is winding its way

Into being,

And although it feels unfamiliar

And a little disconcerting,

You pray for it nevertheless.

You hear the whispers

As it comes closer,

Feel its breath on the back of your neck,

Like a lover,

Reminding you that it is time

To level up.

You are ready to step into the next

More defined

Version of you.

You are ready.

TRUTH - REFLECTIONS & SUMMARY

It has been a deep dive so far, hasn't it? We have initiated ourselves into living our life committed to our Inner Goddess, we have looked at our journey through life so far and the decisions we have made that have led us to where we are now and whether our life still feels aligned or not, and we have focused in quite closely on how we feel about ourselves, particularly on the undercurrent of conscious thoughts that flow constantly within the background of our mind. We have also reconnected to our inner child and reminded her of who she is, what she is capable of, that she is loved and that anything is possible.

Here are a few soul questions for you to reflect on now that you have completed the first Pillar. Notice how your answers might be different now that you have initiated into honouring your Inner Goddess as well as perhaps gaining a deeper perspective on the truth of who you are.

SOUL QUESTIONS

What do you think has been the most significant decision that you have made in your life that has ultimately led you to where you are now?

When you think about why and what influenced you making that decision, does it still resonate with what you believe and want today?

What truth have you identified that you have been telling yourself for too long that is not true?

Do you love and appreciate yourself and your body a little more than you did before your Inner Goddess Initiation?

What areas have you identified that need to change in your life?

PILLAR TWO

ACCEPT

Once you have witnessed and honoured the truth of who you are and your story so far, it is time to move on to the next Pillar, the Pillar of Acceptance. This can be a tough one because you will tend to find that your mind will want to try and drag you back to the past, especially to rake over the things that you wish you should have done and could have done, your mind filling with regret and resentment towards yourself and anyone else involved.

Our mind likes familiar thought patterns which is why we so often feel like we are on a psychological merry-go-round that we can't get off. When we think we have moved on, we are suddenly triggered by something that finds us back in that negative headspace, turning over old stories and blaming ourselves and others for the way things have turned out.

So how do we get to this place of acceptance? How do we make peace with what has been and gone and is? It's really quite simple ... well, it is but it isn't. We remind ourselves that we cannot change what has been and gone or where we are right now, but we can accept that it happened and that those difficulties have given us strength and resilience that we wouldn't have had before. There is a gift within every situation that we can now carry forward with us into the future, stronger for it.

We can now accept that we are in control of how we wish to move forward and what we wish to bring more of or let go of in our life. This is our choice that we can now make.

We can accept that despite what happened in our past, we will not let it define our future unless it is in a positive way that sees us carry the experience as a strength rather than a weakness.

Vigilance is key with our mindset, especially when we are trying to invoke a more positive way of thinking and viewing life and situations, so be mindful when old thought patterns start to creep back in and you perhaps feel yourself falling back into victim mode – which, by the way, is totally human of us. Sometimes a bit of a wallow and a good cry are needed in order to let it out and then pick ourselves up again with the reins in both hands, just as long as we don't stay in wallow mode for too long.

Accepting who we are after we have witnessed our deepest truths works in the same way. If we accept the parts of us that we have always been embarrassed by, then we can live a whole life rather than half of one. Imagine going through the whole of your life and getting to the end only to realise that no one really knew you fully for who you are.

If you can't bring your full self to every situation, every relationship (including the one you have with yourself), then how will you ever experience the fullness of anything? You will only ever live half a life.

THE CALL OF YOUR SOUL IS CONSISTENT

There can be many sides to your personality, but your soul will always remain the same. Its message will always remain the same. Its goal will always remain the same. What it wants from you will always remain the same. Its love for you will always remain the same.

The one constant in your life is your soul which contains the energy, the very unique essence of who you are and the reason that you came here to be you in this lifetime. If you are feeling lost and directionless it is because you are not listening to the calling of your soul. You are ignoring your soul's voice and what it has to say.

If you are feeling frustrated at the lack of communication or guidance from the Universe, you are not listening to your soul's whispers – or perhaps you are, but there is a lack of trust in the connection. You might not like the answer that you are hearing or feeling so you choose to ignore the guidance despite asking for it, and then you wonder why the Universe isn't listening to you, when in fact, it is you that is not listening.

How many versions of you do you feel you have to create in the different circles that you socialise within?

Have you ever asked yourself why you do that? Why you feel the need to close one part of yourself off from certain people?

Is it from fear that they won't understand you, or ridicule that side of your personality?

I can almost guarantee that if you are nodding your head right now, thinking, 'This sounds like me', you have experienced periods of your life when you have still felt the deep ache of loneliness, despite how many people you surround yourself with in life. Perhaps you always feel like you are always standing on the edge of the circle rather than in the middle with everyone else. You are unable to maintain consistent friendships and relationships because you are unable to connect consistently with your soul and its calling.

When you ignore your soul and your connection to it, you will find consistent inconsistencies in every area of your life. You will always find yourself re-visiting the same struggles time and again, going into battle over the same arguments with the same people, attracting the type of people that just don't make you happy. You'll ask yourself why you can't ever seem to get it right, despite hearing your soul's messages every day but choosing to ignore them because it is not what you want to hear or because you simply do not trust your connection to it.

SOUL QUESTIONS

Do you ever feel like the good times in your life just don't last? You can't seem to hang onto them long enough to enjoy them before they disappear?

Explain your answer and give an example of something that came into your life that you couldn't hang onto.

What have you always struggled to be consistent with?

What do you think is happening for this inconsistency to

keep occurring? Where do you think you might be self-sabotaging?

Do you trust your connection to your intuition? Explain your answer.

What do you think you need to do or change in order to find consistency in the inconsistent areas of your life?

EMBRACE THE INNER STORM

When the dark clouds come rolling in, the golden light lost to the shadows, remember to breathe.

When the wind picks up and offers you a sense of foreboding as the rain starts to fall, remember to breathe.

When you sense the urgency rising within you to run for cover and hide, remember to breathe.

Take a moment to consciously connect to the feeling of the coming inner storm.

Do not panic.

Instead, take a moment to relish the gifts that are coming your way.

Can you smell the fresh scent in the air? This is the smell of cleansing, releasing and letting go.

The air feels charged, electric, with the coming purification. There is magic within this magnetic energy.

This is where your dreams are birthed.

This is where the phoenix rises.

How lush and green and fertile does the land feel once the storm has passed?

The green is greener.

The soil is richer.

New beginnings are stirring.

There is a deep, much deeper sense of calm than you have ever experienced before.

You are ready to move forward.

Embrace the inner storm.

AT ONE

Some of us were always meant to walk alone, but if you are truly at one with yourself, you will never feel lonely.

I have spent most of my life standing on the outside looking in, watching others with envy as they bask in the love and support of lifelong friendships and parents whose home they still call 'theirs', drifting back when in need of Mum's home-cooked food and knowing that all the while, they have returned to the nest, however briefly, so that they can un-adult themselves for a while and enjoy being the child again.

Having a base from which to call home, your safety net, your childhood blanket is something that I have never had the pleasure of enjoying.

When I left the RAF and was expecting my first baby, I desperately searched for something to anchor my lost soul onto for fear of always feeling adrift.

I searched for my anchor for a few years as I scrabbled around in the darkness, desperately comparing the lack of love and support in my life with those around me, wondering why it was that I was so alone while others still had their parents to wipe away the tears when life fell apart. I didn't realise that the feeling of love, home and nurture was within me all along.

For the next decade of my life, I focussed daily, religiously, on rebuilding my relationship with myself. Learning to give myself my time and honouring my needs, discovering myself and who I was all over again at 30 years old.

As I dedicated my thirties to self-rediscovery, I built up my business and started saying yes to following my dreams. But as my sense of self grew stronger along with the very essence of my soul, I began to feel smothered and restricted in my marriage.

I battled with the confusion and uncertainty of what I wanted and what no longer felt right for a long time, far too long. I ignored the ever-growing distance between my husband and me. As I aligned my life with my soul's purpose, my personal life began to misalign and unravel.

As I taught and coached my clients and sisterhood members in the art of always following your heart and never ignoring the niggle, my niggle began to grow and consume me as I ignored my own heart.

I felt like a fraud.

I wasn't fully honouring myself and my teachings. Who was I to offer service of self-love and purpose to others when I wasn't fully practising what I was preaching?

One of the deepest worries I had that was holding me back from taking the inevitable step forward was the notion of being alone in my life. Again. I didn't know how to be physically alone because I had always bounced from one relationship to another.

If you have read my first book you will know my story, understanding that my need for a relationship was in fact the need I felt to be anchored, to find my home that I believed would reside in someone else.

I had been with my husband for 15 years and I didn't know how to do life without him, well, adult life that is. There was also the thought that if I walked away from my marriage, I also walked away from my husband's family who had become my family. I would be well and truly on my own with no support network.

I had never relied too heavily upon my in-laws in the past, but the comfort that comes with knowing that they were there if I ever needed them was a comfort.

My dad lives in Qatar and my brother in Kenya, so you see the gravity of my situation.

Deep down, I knew however that fear of being alone was not a good enough reason to stay.

As I battled on through my mid to late thirties, I focussed heavily on pushing the ever-growing niggle back down into the depths of the darkness from which it enjoyed lurking and festering. I continued to follow my intuition in other ways, realising that the fear and indecision that I was faced with meant that I needed to dive much deeper into the inner soul work that I had newly dedicated myself to in order to move past the blockages that I was placing in my own way. I knew that I had to re-discover home within myself all over again.

CDARK NIGHT OF THE SOUL

It was the very end of the summer holidays and the first day that I found myself well and truly pulling and clawing my way out of what had been the longest and one of the hardest transitions of my life. I experienced what many call the 'Dark Night of the Soul' back in 2010 after leaving the RAF and discovering that I was pregnant. The darkness that encapsulated my soul, my spirit, my very essence for a number of years made an appearance again eleven years later on my 39th rotation around the sun when, finally I let go of my 15-year marriage.

I knew it was coming.

I knew that I had to find the courage to step over the edge and let myself fall, but it didn't make the moment any easier when it finally came.

Ironically, after spending a decade dedicated to self-rediscovery after hitting rock bottom in my late twenties, I found myself back in the starting blocks all over again. After all of the work that I had put into myself, the money, the care, the expertise, exploring and honouring every single part of myself so that I might continue to grow and bloom into a stronger, more aligned version of myself with every passing day.

And yet, here it was that I found myself, back at square one. Like time had rewound itself and I found myself back in my 27th year and experiencing the excruciating pain and torture of self-doubt, self-sabotage, debilitating anxiety and bottomless lows.

The other ironic realisation is that I know, I teach, and I understand how the evolution of one's soul unfolds as it travels through lifetime upon lifetime. As a modern Goddess who honours the passing of time and mirrors my own internal seasons with that of Mother Nature's seasons, I know full well that it takes constant re-alignment, re-evaluation and the creation of space for the new to enter in order to continually submit to the daily growth of your soul.

We are ever-evolving, ever-changing, ever-expanding. There is always work to be done when it comes to honouring and maintaining the light of our soul. And yet, this second Dark Night of the Soul still managed to take me by complete surprise and have me questioning why I was experiencing this torture again.

With darkness comes light.

This one line of knowledge, this statement of truth is what I grasped hold of and clung to as I teetered on the edge of oblivion over the summer months of 2021.

What an incredibly eclectic mashup of both the beautiful and the terrible this year had proven itself to be for me. I knew before it arrived that it was going to be a defining and pivotal year for me personally. My debut book was due for release in February, but I also knew that it would be the year that I finally ended my marriage – either that, or something major had to change.

January was a major low as we headed straight into another lockdown and I battled my way through every emotion possible that came with being unable to re-open my business as well as trying to navigate myself and my kids through the ongoing torture of home-schooling.

As we plodded our way through the endless cold and grey misery of January, however, the light at the end of the tunnel was beginning to grow brighter as we headed towards February and the publication of my debut book, *Natural Magic for the Modern Goddess*.

My dream of becoming an author had come true and in the final days of its pre-release, I watched in shock and awe as my book climbed the ranks and made it to best-seller on the day of its launch. I can't tell you the utter euphoria I felt that day and for the weeks that followed afterwards. In fact, I still have to pinch myself two years on. The feedback has been incredible and with every sale, I thank the Universe with everything that I've got that someone else out there is reading my words.

We all rode the wave of euphoria during those weeks after the launch, and for a brief period of time, my husband and I re-connected in a way that we hadn't for a very long time. I felt his support, his passion and commitment to my work and how proud he was that I had followed a childhood dream.

I thought that we had turned a major corner. I thought the Universe had thrown me a curve ball and my marriage was not in fact doomed.

For a while, I felt the deepest sense of inner peace I'd felt in a very long time. I felt whole again. This validation felt like fireworks exploding in every cell of my body. And I felt that it was down to the release of my book, and along with it, many demons and deep-rooted shadows that had haunted me for over a decade. I had finally let it all go and my book had been the catalyst for a change that I knew was coming but had presumed would mean the end of my marriage.

As my husband and I lay in each other's arms one night,

talking and connecting into the small hours of the morning I incredulously (and internally) laughed at how wrong I had been.

This book had been the saviour of my marriage.

But I couldn't have been more wrong.

It was to bring the final chapter on this path in my life to a close, once and for all.

Soul Questions

Have you experienced a Dark Night of the Soul? A time of despair, loss, pain, a debilitating period of time when your soul felt like it was cracking open? Write about your experiences and how it made you feel.

What were you scared or worried about at the time?

How much of what you worried would happen, did happen?

What strengths did your Dark Night give you that you did not realise at the time, but appreciate now?

What transformation occurred within you and your life after this?

Take a moment to send a silent prayer of gratitude out to the Universe, as well as to yourself for how far you have come.

THE BEGINNING OF THE END

I look back on that final night that my husband and I shared together as a beautiful way of saying goodbye, despite not realising that's was what it was at the time.

Shortly afterwards, I felt a palpable and unexplainable shift between us that came out of nowhere. It felt like the key had finally turned in the lock to a very heavy oak door.

I simply woke up one morning and knew that it was over. Our journey together had reached its natural end and it was time to let go.

The initial weeks of separation were painful for us all, but for me, it wasn't an unbearable pain because deep down I knew that I had made the right decision. However, two months after separating, my world came crashing down around me. My mind began to fill with all-consuming anxiety and fear for the unknown that lay ahead of me. All the 'what-ifs' and 'how on Earth I was going to survive on my own' weighed so heavy that I felt like I was drowning under the weight of it all.

I questioned everything, including my sanity.

The question mark that up-skittled me the most however was the one I now placed upon my work. My work had always been my anchor, my reason, my sanity, and now I found myself questioning the one thing in my life that I had always known to be true above all else.

I lost every foundation.

I was anchorless.

I was starting to drown.

Not only that, but I had to try and drown in silence with as little disruption to my girls as I could possibly muster.

THE PAIN IS THE MAGIC

To immerse yourself fully into honouring your Inner Goddess, there is absolutely no escaping the fact that with life comes pain. There is no way of skirting your life around it, the only way to deal with it is to meet it head-on and immerse yourself fully in the rich, dark and jagged edges of it while it ravages your body, mind and soul.

To surrender to pain in all its forms is to accept that there will be a part of you that will never be the same. There will be a part of you that will feel like you have died. You will wonder if you will ever recover, if you will ever be or feel the same again. You will tear yourself apart with the torment of ifs and buts, should-haves and could-haves.

But with pain comes truth.

With pain comes honesty.

With pain comes clarity.

With pain comes strength, a strength to eventually gather up the broken pieces of yourself from amongst the dirt and darkness.

Pain gives you fire in your belly and a deeper sense of self-preservation and understanding of what you truly desire and deserve.

With pain comes formidable boundaries that will stand taller and more stead-fast with every tidal wave that attempts to crash into them.

Pain not only makes us stronger but also softens us in order to empathise with others who are struggling with their pain. It gives us a reason to unite and support one another. It shows us that we are not alone despite how lonely and isolating being in pain can be.

Pain gives us duality to pleasure. We can only truly appreciate moments of pleasure when we have experienced moments of pain.

The more pain that we experience, the wiser we become. We are able to appreciate that nothing lasts forever and that eventually the painful times will pass and we will feel stronger and more connected to life and our place within it than ever before.

The biggest lessons and gifts come from the most painful experiences.

I have learnt to search for that delicious golden thread of painful growth and new beginnings within the darkest moments in my life. It is within these moments that I often step into 'observer' and witness that I am experiencing the pain of deep release, an ending of a chapter, and preparing myself for a new one that has been waiting patiently for me to birth it into being.

It may sound strange but there is an undercurrent of excitement and trepidation deep within me during the darkest experiences with pain. I also feel it when I witness my friends or even my clients hit rock bottom. of course, I can empathise and find myself wishing that I could stop the pain for them, but I also see these pivotal moments as a major period of transformation right before the butterfly emerges once more and life explodes with more gifts than could ever be imagined at the time.

Soul Question

Think back to a painful experience and how you felt at the time you were going through it, unaware that life would eventually turn a corner for the better and you would be happier than you ever thought possible. What gifts came into your life as a result of this painful experience?

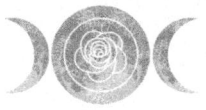

YOU ARE A MASTERPIECE

Those old stories,
Fears and doubts
Are reminding you to let go.
Breeeeathe.
Let your muscles relax,
Let go of fear, doubt, worry, anxiety,
Not-good-enough,
Not loveable enough...
You are a master,
A master at being you.
No one knows you and what makes you tick,
What lights you up,
What brings you joy,
What gives you strength
Like you do.
No one knows how deep
The well of strength, resilience, and determination
goes within you.
No one knows how thick the armour is
That you have crafted

From hard and painful lessons
You've been through in this lifetime
And beyond.
You are a masterpiece created from it all.
There is no one else like you.
So, take those old stories
And thank them for creating a masterpiece...
And let them go.
It's time for the next chapter,
The next layer of wisdom to be gathered,
The next piece of armour to be added,
The inner well of strength and resilience
And determination to be dug
Even deeper.
It's time to open your heart even wider.

ACCEPT - REFLECTIONS & SUMMARY

Accepting the truth of where you are and how you came to be here in this moment with your life experiences can be one of the hardest of the five Goddess Pillars to work with. To accept everything that has ever happened to you, especially the difficult and painful things, means that you have to make your peace with it. You have to accept the injustice and you have to commit to taking full responsibility from now on for your life and your happiness despite what has happened in the past.

To accept is to let go of blame or guilt or shame or thoughts of not being enough. To let go means that you can no longer hide behind these feelings and use them as an excuse for not living your life the way that you really want.

To accept is to own it all, the good, the bad and the ugly and consciously choose to move forward with your life without defining or feeling defined by your past.

In this section, I have shared with you how the call of your soul is consistent in the way that it nudges you until you listen and accept what is really meant for you. We have talked about embracing and accepting some of the toughest times in our lives and how to look out for the golden thread that offers us the gift within these difficult experiences. We have identified times in our life when we may have experienced a Dark Night of the Soul and that hindsight has shown us the strength that we have gained from these painful experiences. Lastly, we have revisited and danced with 'pain' and how to not only sink into these dark and painful moments but also to hold onto the glimmer of light and hope that something beautiful will come as a result of this pain.

Now that we have connected to our Acceptance Goddess Pillar, here are some questions for you to consider.

Who do you feel you have to hide your true self from when you are with them?

Do you think it is about them not accepting you, or you not accepting yourself?

Do you enjoy spending time with yourself? Do you feel most at home with yourself? Explain your answer.

When you think about potentially experiencing another Dark Night of the Soul, do you feel scared or do you now see these dark moments as a time of realignment and transformation?

Think about a painful experience. How did it bring clarity and truth to your life? How did you build yourself up again stronger than before?

PILLAR THREE

HEAL

The Healing Pillar of Goddess is where the real journey begins. Now it is time to do the work, to get really up close and personal with yourself, and this can be a really uncomfortable place to be.

There are so many layers to healing and sometimes we have to return to a layer that we thought we had already healed because the pain and the trauma run deeper than we realised. Healing is not a quick fix or a one-time visit. Healing can be something that you may have to work on for the rest of your life. In fact, because our mind loves familiar thought patterns and routines, it may find us back at the Acceptance Pillar once again because we have become so used to our mind processing and storing its trauma in the way that it has always done.

But know that if you are committed to your healing and your future, you will heal and you will be able to move on with your life.

As you will discover in this section, healing may take you deep into the history of your childhood, or perhaps even further back into the trauma that your ancestors carried that has passed down through the generations to you. You will learn about the concept of karma and the lessons that you have brought with you from previous lifetimes. You will learn how to identify the different shadows that you may face and how to re-frame them as well as understand the power of the womb as a portal for healing ancestral trauma.

This dive is deep, so take your time, there is no rush. Sit with what comes up for you for as long as it takes for you to feel the acceptance and the release. A healing journey is a powerful journey, everything must be witnessed so if you can, create some sacred and private space while you work through this section, in particular the Shadow Work, Womb Healing and Triple Goddess Healing.

A THOUSAND STARS

A thousand stars twinkle
in the dark spaces
where your soul has cracked.
You are unaware of their presence,
Your eyes shut tightly
Against the pain of it all.
As you take in a breath,
The stars glow brighter.
Keep breathing, my love,
You are breathing your way
To wholeness.
You don't feel like you are,
But trust that you are.
If only you knew
What lay beneath,
A thousand more stars that fill your soul,
Each one a gift,
A lesson, a journey,
Pain, beauty, a thousand lifetimes
Of heartbeats

Waiting to be uncovered,
To shine through the darkness.
If only you knew.
Your pain is yet another star
Being birthed into your soul,
Another twinkle to add to your rich tapestry.
A thousand stars twinkle
In the dark spaces
Where your soul has cracked.
You are unaware of their presence,
But they shine brightly for you,
They shine so very strong for you,
Each a witness to your birth,
Your death, your re-birth.
Each star is you,
And you are each and every star.
As you lay in your cloak of darkness,
Afraid you will lose yourself to it all,
Another star is born
And you are shining brighter
Than ever before.

THE OBSERVER - MY SAVIOUR

My Dark Night of the Soul had arrived and with it a virus that knocked me off my feet for nearly a month. I knew that it was coming. I felt it building. I tried to ignore it and push through it. I kept my mind and my body pushing and moving forward despite the exhaustion that I could feel settling deep into my bones and my psyche.

I stopped writing and journaling.

I stopped communicating consciously with my guides.

The feeling of being anchorless was once again upon me as I drifted aimlessly through the summer days that should have been enjoyed with the kids.

What was worse was the huge question mark that now lingered over my work. How could this be? My work was the very thing that anchored me and my purpose to my soul.

Why did I feel such a sudden severance from it? Why did I feel like everything was such an effort? A chore?

Why did I want to give it all up and run away from my life?

I was of course shedding the old to make way for the new. I was transitioning into the next chapter of my life. I was re-aligning my soul with my purpose. I was in a deep, dark cocoon of transformation, and despite the days when the anxiety and the darkness of uncertainty consumed me, I understood exactly where I was. I knew that the only way through it was through it.

I knew that the butterfly was preparing to emerge and that something beautiful was coming. And so it was that I surrendered to it all in the best way that I knew how to.

During the darkest days, I taught myself to mindfully step back and to simply observe where I was at. Stepping back outside of myself helped me to look at my situation from a different perspective, the perspective of the observer with a detachment from the pain.

It helped me to step back and take deep lungfuls of air when I thought that I couldn't breathe.

Becoming the observer was my saviour.

SOUL QUESTION

Is there a situation that you are struggling with that you could consciously try to step back from and become the observer?

DO NOT ALLOW YOURSELF TO BE
DEFINED BY OTHER'S EXPECTATIONS

SHADOW WORK

In order to fully integrate and initiate into your Inner Goddess, you must commit to diving deep into a lifelong love affair with the deepest, darkest parts of you. Not in an obsessive way that keeps you locked in the past, but in a nurturing way that takes care of your ever-evolving soul throughout your lifetime.

Shadow Work is so very important. Not only does it help to release karmic patterns that imprint from lifetime to lifetime, but it also helps us to understand ourselves on a soul level, on a spiritual and energetic level. When acknowledged for the lessons that these shadows have taught us, only then are we able to move forwards and stop making the same mistakes over and over again in our relationships, in our jobs and with life decisions and choices that we make.

These shadows that I talk about are the parts of us that we struggle with the most. The parts of us that keep us small, feeling unloved and believing false truths about ourselves and others.

Shadows leave us with feelings of less-than, unworthy, not good enough, anger, bitterness, and unable to let go of people and experiences that have wronged us in some way.

When shadows are left to fester, undealt with, they rot and settle into the core of us, becoming a force of destruction, pain and relentless hopelessness.

However, what so many of us do not realise as we desperately try to ignore our shadows, pushing them away each and every time they come clawing to the surface, is that each one contains a beautiful gift, a gift for our soul to discover and learn from in this lifetime.

When we take the time to crack open the dark shell, we will discover a beautiful gold thread passing and weaving its way through the centre. This gold thread contains alignment, clarity, renewed purpose, a deeper sense of love and understanding for who we are, appreciation, gratitude, peace, and ultimately the next positive step along our soul's journey of growth. This gold thread is a life lesson that will help to shape and create another beautiful facet of the eternal part of you – your beautiful soul.

Let's take a look at the different types of shadow that you may have already encountered or perhaps are unfamiliar with.

KARMIC SHADOW

The word karma originates in Hinduism and Buddhism, meaning, *'the sum of a person's actions in this and previous states of existence, viewed as deciding their fate in future existences'.* oxfordreference.com 2006

There is a belief by many and in cultures such as Hinduism and Buddhism that we return many times over to this planet to experience lessons that will shape our soul from lifetime to lifetime. If a lesson has been left unfinished before we pass back to Source at the end of each lifetime, or perhaps not fully grasped or understood, we will come back to attempt to teach ourselves again in future lifetimes.

An example of a Karmic Lesson is when we continually choose to share our life with people who do not make us happy and do not treat us well. If you have ever experienced past life regression you will more than likely discover during your regression that there is a link between yourself and the person that you are struggling with from a previous lifetime. This person may well continue to return time and again with you, incarnating into a new life and treating you in a similar way because you have not learnt the lesson from this relationship in this, or previous lifetimes.

You have more than likely spent a lifetime in which you were too afraid to leave that person or situation, or perhaps you did but left with unresolved trauma, unable to find acceptance, release or gratitude for the life lesson that you were gifted from this person/situation.

When you pass over, returning to Source, you choose to re-learn the lesson again when you return into a new life so that you can release the associated karma with the unresolved lesson.

The Karmic Shadow comes in many forms, but the most common is that you continue to attract the same negative people or situations into your life without understanding why or where you are going wrong.

You may perhaps experience a deep, emotional pain, fear or in fact any negative response to a person or situation that you struggle to understand because you cannot find a root cause in this lifetime to justify your response and how you feel.

A friend once told me that from as early as she could remember she had a deep fear of snow. Living in the Highlands of Scotland did of course absolutely nothing to settle this seemingly irrational fear. She eventually decided to try past life regression, only to discover that, in a previous life she was left out in the snow as a baby to die because her parents were too poor to feed her. During the session, the therapist helped her soul to revisit this past-life memory and find a peace that helped her to release the karma from this situation. Her fear of snow disappeared. The Karmic Shadow was finally released and will no longer return to her in any future lifetime.

CURRENT SUBCONSCIOUS SHADOW

These are the shadows that we have created in this lifetime or have entered our subconscious from an outside source, imprinting into our psyche in subtle but also extreme ways.

Current Subconscious Shadows manifest from unresolved trauma surrounding a negative experience that we have had in our past. Many CSS stem from our childhood and experiences that impacted so heavily on our young mind that we did not/ could not process it at the time. Perhaps we developed a coping mechanism by teaching our mind to block the memory of it out so that we go on to spend years afterwards believing that we are over it until, one day, something supposedly unrelated happens to cause a trigger in our memory and we lash out or experience an unexplained eruption of emotion.

With CSS it can often be quite a challenge to uncover the root cause of the behavioural issue or sudden depression/worry/ anxiety that you may now be experiencing seemingly out of nowhere and far beyond your conscious comprehension. You struggle to understand why you feel the way that you do, having no idea how to go about making yourself well again first before visiting the doctor who will, inevitably, offer you medication without attempting to find the root cause.

With CSS, the very best advice that I can offer you is to seek support from the variety of supportive therapists out there. Recommendations are always a wonderful way of choosing a therapy and therapist, but remember that what works for one does not necessarily always work for another. Don't be afraid to try different things in order to find the therapy method that works best for you.

A form of Hypnotherapy might be the way forward for you because it is a wonderful way of helping you to reach the parts of your subconscious mind that hold the memories that you perhaps have forgotten were there, or might not have pinpointed its association to the CSS that have now been triggered.

Forms of Hypnotherapy such as Neurolinguistic Programming (NLP) are exceptional from my personal experience at providing practical ways in which you can change the way that you think and review past-life events, helping you to re-frame the memory and take back positive control of your mind.

Search 'NLP in my area' online to find your nearest practitioner.

CURRENT CONSCIOUS SHADOWS

The journey from acknowledging CCS to healing them can often be much shorter than with Karmic and Subconscious Shadows because we already know where the trauma/trigger originates from. We hold the memory within our mind with a full awareness of its presence.

With the rise in awareness and the release of social stigmas associated with mental health, we are becoming a lot more open to considering therapy and recognising the triggers/shadows within our mental health than we have ever been before.

Acknowledgment and acceptance are the first keys to unlocking the door to all Shadow Work, and you will once again discover a plethora of therapies and support networks out there to help you work through these shadows.

Current Conscious Shadows will make you feel like you are on a merry-go-round that you can't get off. The shadow will pop up regularly at unexpected moments, triggered by a word, a smell, a situation or person. Or it may have perhaps become all-consuming, taking over your life so that you are unable to function and think straight. All shadow types have the ability to control your mind in this way. They are what keep us trapped, small, frightened, unable to break free of negative and abusive people and situations.

Somewhere along the way, these shadows became regular, unquestioned, permanent fixtures. Somewhere along the way you have accepted their presence and allowed them to take up permanent residency, festering away and causing havoc and a silent inner destruction.

When you picked up this book and chose to read it, I believe this was because you are at a point in your journey along the sacred spiral of life in which you feel that you have lost the connection to who you are, to your Inner Goddess – or perhaps you feel that you have never met her because she has never been allowed to step forwards and shine.

Life can become so busy and tiring with responsibilities and commitments that it can so often become inevitable that we start to wander for periods of time, feeling disconnected and disillusioned with our life and where we now find ourselves.

Somewhere along the way you have told yourself that it is OK to slowly give pieces of yourself away because it'll keep the peace, it's the right thing to do, it is what is expected, you will not be loved if you do what you really want to do. Ultimately, you are not at the top of your own pile.

Initiating your Inner Goddess isn't just about celebrating the good things and committing time to the fun stuff. It is also about the love and the care and the time that we honour ourselves with each and every day, as we face our shadows head-on and continue to commit to raising our Inner Goddess up out of the darkness and into the light.

Our human life is about balance. In fact, the whole of creation and all that exists is here and existing because it has struck a balance between light and dark, life and death, health and dis-ease. Without one there is no other, just a constant of the same, and there are gifts on each side of the fence.

It is OK to experience both the dark and the light. This is part of what it means to be Divinely Human.

SHADOW WORK INVESTIGATION

Let us delve deeper now into understanding some of the shadows that you might be dealing with in this lifetime in order to take the first step – acknowledgment – on the sacred ladder to healing them once and for all.

It is important to choose a time to focus on these questions when you will not be disturbed. Being in a place of privacy will help you to relax and to feel safe to express emotions that will rise to the surface for releasing.

Do you feel that you carry shadows with you in this lifetime that create a negative impact on your life?

Without considering what these shadows are yet, or where they come from, describe the negative emotion/feeling/experience/situation that these shadows manifest as in your life.

Have you been aware of the shadows and their recurring presence before reading this chapter? Or are you just starting to connect some dots?

If you have recognised the presence of shadows in your life before now, explain when and how it was that you first became aware of them.

Do your shadows have a recurring pattern, triggered by the same or similar situations? Or are their appearances sporadic in nature?

If you could rate your shadows from 1-10 in severity – 10 being the most severe impact on your life – what rating would you give them?

Do you think that the effect/impact that the shadows are having on your life has gotten worse over time, better, or stayed the same? Explain.

If you have only just connected your conscious awareness to shadows, explain why you think you did not pay them much attention before now.

Knowing what you know now about Karmic, Subconscious and Conscious Shadows, what would you possibly class your shadows as?

If you think you know where your shadows stem from, write the circumstances of how they came to be here.

Making the connection, knowing what you know now and understanding why, do you feel able to able to respond to it in an empowered way on your own moving forward for any future recurrence? Or do you feel like you might need extra support and guidance from a therapist or doctor? Explain your answer.

What do you believe will be the positive impact now that you understand the root cause of your shadows?

If you feel that you need more in-depth support, which therapy mentioned in this chapter do you feel might be a good place to start for supporting you? If unsure, set out some time to learn more about the one that you are drawn to before arranging an appointment.

If you were to leave the shadows untouched, how do you think they might continue to impact your life in a negative way?

CRE-FRAME YOUR SHADOW MEDITATION FOR CURRENT CONSCIOUS SHADOWS

Follow this link to recordings of the meditations in this book! https://tinyurl.com/IOGoddess

Find somewhere comfortable to lie or sit down. Make sure that your back is straight.

Close your eyes and take some deep breaths in through the nose, filling your lungs up to the very top before releasing all the air out through your mouth. Do this two or three times, feeling your body relax and your energy settle into your body.

You are safe to be exactly where you are right now.

Allow any remaining tension to flow down to your feet and out through the soles.

Breathe.

I want you to imagine that you are standing in the middle of a lush green field on a warm summer's day. Your feet are bare, and you can feel the warm grass beneath you. As you look around the meadow you see hundreds of beautiful wildflowers bobbing their heads merrily in the soft summer breeze, and you take a breath in, feeling the sun on your skin, completely and utterly relaxed.

You turn your face up to the sun and gaze at the beautiful, soft blue sky dotted with white, fluffy clouds. You start to feel yourself gently lifting off the ground, but you are not concerned. You trust that the Universe is looking after you as you rise higher and higher into the sky, coming to rest on a beautiful, big, soft cloud.

As you snuggle into it, the cloud wraps itself around you like a soft blanket and you close your eyes as you begin to drift through the sky, safe and comfortable.

You allow the cloud to drift and float, float and drift, carrying you gently through the sky, wrapped up in a blanket of cotton wool.

The cloud passes over fields and valleys, mountains and lakes, as time begins to unwind as you drift and float, relaxed and safe.

You are being taken back to a time, a place, a memory that has been left unfinished. You are travelling back in order to heal.

You are safe and content within your cloud.

No harm will come to you as you re-visit the memory, simply a different perspective will be gifted to you in order to release the shadow and its influence on your current life.

The cloud begins to slow and descend gently towards the Earth below. As you get lower and lower you continue to breathe deeply, deep and calming breaths, safe and secure.

As the cloud reaches the ground you gently lift yourself up and off, your feet planting firmly on the floor. As you look around you the scene is familiar. It is the scene from your memory. You have seen it many times before in your mind.

Is there anybody else there with you? Are you alone?

What can you see, hear, touch, smell?

Remember, you are only observing this memory.

You are just the observer.

Observe the memory of yourself in this moment.

Remember how you felt at the time.

Did you get the chance to speak your truth to someone? If not, now is the time to say everything that you needed to say.

Tell them how you feel and what you are thinking.

Let them know that their opinions are their own and that you do not carry the responsibility of them.

Thank them for the lessons that they have taught you.

Tell them that it is now time for you to walk a separate path of love and peace as they walk and drift out of focus into the distance.

If you are by yourself, allow your thoughts to move forward to the moment that creates the future shadow. What happens in this scene?

How does it end?

How do you feel?

You are now able to re-frame the ending. What would need to change in this situation in order for you to move forward with your life untethered from its negative influence?

What would you do differently?

Change the outcome. If you felt fear, worry, or anxiety, for example, imagine yourself stepping back from that situation with a clear and calm mind.

As the familiar feelings and emotions rise within this memory, ask yourself how you would like to feel instead and feel it.

Accept the situation for what it was because you are now free to leave it in the past.

Imagine that you are taking a large pair of scissors and cutting the large, dark cord that connects this shadow to you.

Repeat the words:

I release myself

Of all energetic ties to... (your CCS)

Real or imagined.

This (CCS) no longer controls me.

The energy and influence are severed.

The cord is cut.

I am now at peace.

I accept the lessons learnt

And move forward with grace.

I feel light and free

And whole again,

To choose my path forward

Once more.

Breathe.

When you feel that you are ready, turn back towards the way that you came when you entered the memory, feeling the weightlessness in your shoulders, your energy lighter.

As you move towards the cloud, you smile, grateful you came as you climb on and sink soft and snug into it, wrapping its softness around you, tucking yourself right into its core.

Gently the cloud begins to rise, heading back the way it came, over the hills, rivers, mountains and valleys.

The longer that you are snuggled down within the cloud, the lighter you feel as time and distance move you further away from the memory that you have visited.

Breathe and relax.

You feel full of light.

You feel so relaxed.

Soon the cloud starts to descend, slowly moving down, down, down until it reaches the Earth.

You gently sit up and climb out of the cloud, planting your feet firmly on the ground.

You are back in the beautiful meadow, surrounded by hundreds of stunning wildflowers.

I am now going to count you back from five to one. When I reach one, you will find yourself back in your body, back in the present moment.

Five, four, three, two, one.

You are back in the room, in the present moment and you start to move your body, your fingers and toes.

Open your eyes and stretch!

You may want to grab a glass of water and your journal.

Make a note of how you are feeling.

Write down how you have reframed your shadow.

Any time that you feel it creeping in again at the edges of your mind, remember to step back, take a deep, calming breath and replay how you re-framed it.

Feel the lightness that comes with the memory now.

WOMB HEALING &
ANCESTRAL TRAUMA

Two years ago I returned to the sacred lands of Avalon in Somerset to dive deeper than I had ever gone before into the study and practice of healing ancestral trauma through Shamanic Womb Healing.

I had booked myself onto a five-day immersive course facilitated by the incredible Angie Twydall, and by the time I left Glastonbury to return home, I found myself unable to find the words to explain to friends what I had experienced that week. Assisting in the healing of the womb space required that I too had to initiate my own womb healing and I knew it was going to be BIG! How could it not?

Healing the womb means healing the wounds and traumas and old stories that have been passed down to us through our lineage from our mother, her mother, her mother before that and so on as well as our own shadows that we carry with us in this lifetime and from past lives.

The stories that we carry from one generation to another are as old as time. They are the reason that we become stuck in cyclical negative patterns and behaviours. If we find ourselves repeating the same stories as our mother then we must definitely alert ourselves to the fact that we are living with unresolved ancestral trauma.

Muscle holds memory. How many times have you heard someone tell their friend, partner, or sister to try and stay calm and relaxed during pregnancy so that the baby remains calm and safe and relaxed? If Mum is stressed, the baby will feel stressed.

Our experience of gestation within our mother's womb is believed to be stored deep within our subconscious. We won't remember a single moment of the nine months in utero but that doesn't mean that the memories aren't there, stored within the parts of our brain that we struggle to access consciously.

There is more and more focus on the connection that our physical body has to the thoughts, feelings and emotions that are stored within the brain and how our body becomes what we think by manifesting that thought or emotion in a physical way that often we simply can't ignore. It is therefore absolutely feasible in my opinion that memories of old stories and trauma held within the fibres and muscles of our mother are passed onto us while she carries us within her.

Holistic healing is very much centred around healing the whole of a person, not just the physical because so often, there is a root psychological cause that plays a major part in the manifestation of a physical complaint/disease of the body. You may want to recap the chapter 'Decode Your Body's Messages' from *Natural Magic for the Modern Goddess* to learn about how some specific emotions and their origins are often found to be linked to certain problematic areas of physical health.

What I learnt fundamentally from my time with Angie and the other trainee shamanic womb practitioners is that the womb space itself is believed to be the seat or the sacred well that holds all of our stories and the stories of those that have come before us. The womb is the portal of life, the place where we first come into existence and the place from which we physically enter into the world.

If we heal our womb space, healing within every other area of our health and wellbeing will follow. We will heal generations of trauma and karma that would otherwise continue to repeat themselves within each generation and/or current lifetime. This healing allows the next generation to live a life of freedom to create their own stories, healing and growth.

What I absolutely adored about my Shamanic Womb Healing training was the beautiful mix of magic that we were taught that wove a balance of the shamanistic, spiritual journeying and visualising with the practical hands-on healing approach that supports clients with physical complaints and problematic areas of their feminine health.

While journeying with our clients into their past as well as through timelines that went back further still, we supported and encouraged the return of physical homeostasis (balance/equilibrium) back to the body with physical therapeutic touch and massage.

Do you suffer or have ever suffered with your feminine health? For example, painful periods, polycystic ovaries, fibroids, irregular cycles, and menopause? I can highly recommend that the next decision that you make be to find a Womb Healing Practitioner who can help you bring your mind and body back to equilibrium. If you suffer from physical complaints of the reproductive system, my belief is that you are holding on to unresolved emotional issues, stories and trauma. It's time to free yourself of it all and create a new chapter in your story.

It is important to mention here that womb healing can be offered to souls who no longer have a womb. The energy and trauma is still stored within the pelvic space where your womb once was.

So, how can we help support ourselves further as part of our beautiful journey back to reconnecting with our Inner Goddess? Offering my clients self-help techniques is one of the best and most successful ways of supporting beautiful women, but more importantly, being able to hand them back the reins to their life, their health and their sense of self again offers the most fierce and incredible sense of empowerment.

You can combine elements of these techniques with elements of the Triple Goddess Womb Healing Ritual from *Natural Magic for the Modern Goddess* if you feel drawn intuitively to do so. However you choose to support and heal your Inner Goddess, as long as it feels good for you then you will never get it wrong.

Please be mindful that if you are in any pain or discomfort to use your intuition and stop and always seek medical advice where appropriate.

These techniques are NOT SUITABLE FOR PREGNANCY.

You may want to create your own beautiful blend of supportive, balancing and tonic-inducing essential oils to use on your tummy and reflex points. This blend is the same blend from the Triple Goddess Womb Healing Ritual. Here it is again for you.

You will need:-

Rose (*Rosa centifolia*) PURE essential oil

Geranium (*Pelargonium graveolens*) PURE essential oil

50mls of sunflower, coconut or sweet almond oil

Add 15 drops of geranium and 5 drops of rose to 50mls of your carrier oil and shake well.

Geranium essential oil properties – refreshing and relaxing, balances hormones and lifts the spirit. Stimulates the lymphatic and reproductive system. Reduces anxiety and stress.

Rose essential oil properties – uterine tonic, cleanses and regulates uterine activity. Reduces premenstrual tension and painful/heavy periods. Relieves tension.

As I mentioned earlier, you can include these techniques as part of your Triple Goddess Womb Healing Ritual or separately on their own if you haven't quite got enough time for a bath, crystals and an entire ritual process. It is however important that you don't rush your healing self-care. Take your time and find somewhere where you won't be disturbed, somewhere where you can sit or lie down comfortably.

You may want to place a towel around or underneath you if you are using oil.

Squeeze a small amount of the oil onto your palm and massage it gently onto your stomach from the bottom of the ribs down to just above your pubic bone. Massage the oil in circular clockwise motions until all of the skin is covered. Rub the oil into your hands and around your wrists too. You are ready to begin.

Reproductive Massage & Healing Ritual

Settle yourself and close your eyes.

Take some deep grounding breaths with one hand over your heart and the other over your womb space.

As you breathe in, imagine that you are breathing into your heart. As you breathe out, imagine that you are carrying your breath from your heart down into your womb space. With each breath in and out you are creating a beautiful connection between your heart and your womb. They are connecting with each other. They are honouring the truths that lay hidden within their sacred space.

When you feel ready, gently massage the whole of your tummy in a soft, clockwise motion. You are covering the whole space between your pubic bone and the bottom of your rib cage. As you do, imagine that you are stirring the sacred energies of your womb space. Imagine that you are opening up the portal to your lineage with a beautiful spiral of energy that gathers and swirls as you circle your abdomen. Choose a colour for the energy that you are creating. Perhaps a colour has already come into your mind.

Breathe and know that you are safe and you are held by your Inner Goddess, your guides and angels.

Now take your left hand, and with your palm down, let your fingers find the hollow below your sternum at the centre of your chest. This is where your ribs join together.

Apply a gentle pressure and move your fingers straight down from your sternum to just above your belly button.

Now with your palm flat, massage around your lower abdomen in a clockwise direction, down to the inside of your left hip bone, across your lower abdomen, over your womb space to just inside your right hip bone, up and back over your tummy just above your belly button.

Move your fingers back up to the hollow just under your sternum and repeat the massage.

Do this 4 or 5 times.

While you massage your body, it is important to keep your mind focused softly on your intention that you wish to create. You may wish to create a short mantra to repeat out loud or quietly within your mind such as, '*I let go of all emotions, old stories and pain that no longer serve me. I invite in my deepest truth, love and healing*'.

Now move your left hand down with your fingers resting just inside your left hip bone over your ovary space. Use your fingers to gently massage in a clockwise motion for 10 seconds before moving across to just above your pubic bone over your womb space. Massage at a depth that is comfortable for you in a clockwise motion for ten seconds.

Now move over to just inside your right hip crease and work over your ovary space in the same way as your right.

Now come up the right side of your abdomen and circle back around, just above your belly button, down your left side, across your pelvic area and back up your right side. Continue to massage your abdomen 4 or 5 times.

Now go back to massaging the ovary spaces and the womb space again, followed by the full circle of the abdomen.

You want to complete each cycle 3 times.

Keep your intention and your mantra in your mind.

Let yourself feel the emotions that may rise from within you as your body lets go and releases the old stories.

Let your tears flow if they beg to fall.

Know that your healing is working and love yourself even more deeply for the care and attention and love that you are showing yourself right now.

Finish your womb massage the way that you started. Place your fingers at the hollow below your sternum, apply pressure and move them down to just above your belly button. Massage around your abdomen in a clockwise direction and move back up to your sternum.

Repeat 4 or 5 times.

To finish, place both of your palms over your womb space and hold for a minute. Let all your love and healing pour into yourself.

You now want to work around your wrists for a little extra support from a reflexology perspective.

Reflexology is the application of pressure to specific points known as reflexes on the hands, feet and face that are believed to correspond with the organs, systems and structures of the body. Reflexologists believe that by stimulating a reflex, they are stimulating the corresponding area of the body to re-introduce balance and harmony.

The ovary and uterus reflexes are located in the little grooves underneath the wrist bones. With your middle finger resting in the dip underneath the outside wrist bone (ovary) and your thumb simultaneously resting in the dip underneath the inside wrist bone (uterus) you can simply apply a gentle holding link for 20 seconds. Repeat your mantra and your intention as you do.

In reflexology, we work the right side of the body first and then the left. The right represents the past and the left represents the present. Once you have finished on your right wrist, work your left.

Place one hand on your heart and the other over your womb space and finish with a few cycles of heart/womb breathing.

Give yourself as much time as you need to sit up. Make your movements slow and measured. Drink some water and grab your journal.

What came up for you?

What emotions rose from within you?

Did old memories come flooding in ready to be released?

Write about your experience with love and gratitude for it all. Honour the lessons and the strength that came with the pain and know that you have now closed a chapter (or several) and you are ready to create some new stories.

It's important to mention here that everyone's healing journey is different and can vary in the time it takes to feel healed. Working on ourselves is a constant journey and commitment to checking in with where we are at. Our mind loves repetition and being able to pull us back to the familiar. This is why we find it so hard to kick bad habits. With this in mind, be prepared to carry out your womb healing ritual often for as long as it takes. You may want to consider making it a part of your monthly self-care routine and include it within the beautiful Triple Goddess Womb Healing Ritual. Give yourself a whole evening of indulgence, relaxation and healing.

We are always a work in progress.

We are always learning, evolving and healing.

CRETURNING LIGHT

When the light slowly begins to return, filtering its way through the cracks in your mind, you sense it with fleeting moments of hope and a lightness to your heart, so slight that if you're not careful, you might miss it.

Seven days after my darkest night of the soul in which I experienced the very worst of the debilitating anxiety, I woke one morning expecting the familiar wave of nauseous anxiety to attack before settling like a heavy brick within the pit of my stomach, but it wasn't there. Instead, there was a sense of something else.

What was it? Hope?

It felt familiar and strong. It felt like it connected me in a very subtle way back to myself and Source.

I took a deep breath in and felt a calmness settle over me like a blanket. I tentatively opened my laptop to start creating my weekly content for the Natural Me Sisterhood and I dove into it with a re-ignited love and passion that I had missed, that I had lacked these past few weeks.

As I acknowledged the sacred feeling of returning, I experienced another most precious of gifts from a Goddess who has always returned to me when I have needed her most.

AN APPEARANCE FROM MY GODDESS, BRIGID

For those of you who know my story, you will be familiar with my relationship with Brigid.

Brigid is the Celtic Goddess of Fire, the Forge, the Hearth, Poetry, Healing, Childbirth, Unity and Smithcraft, and she first appeared to me at the very start of my spiritual journey.

At the time of my first encounter with Brigid, I knew nothing of her and yet, when she appeared to me in a meditation/vision one day, I felt an instant recognition of familiarity and love for this red-headed woman that I had never before met.

So profound was my experience that I could not get her out of my mind. Over the days that passed I started to feel into the energy that still lingered from her presence and knew that she had to be an ancient deity. When I googled 'red-haired Goddess', her image appeared a hundred times over and I felt the pulse of electric energy pass through my body and into the deepest recesses of my soul.

I had found her. I knew who she was, and I knew that I wasn't wrong as I read and learnt about one of the most loved and revered Goddesses, who was also made a saint. Brigid's Day is celebrated on the 2nd of February, a day also known as Imbolc which marks the halfway point between winter and spring.

Our ancient ancestors would celebrate this most auspicious of days as the Wheel of the Year continued to turn and the arrival of spring and new beginnings was imminent.

When I read the date – the 2nd of February – I knew that Brigid was the Goddess who had visited me because it was only four days before Imbolc arrived.

As I learnt about the Goddess of Motherhood, Childbirth and New Beginnings I began to connect the dots to so many synchronicities that had happened over the years in my life around Imbolc.

I met my husband and the father of my children on the 2nd of February. I had conceived both of my children during Imbolc. I had lost my son on Imbolc, and I had birthed my book into the world on Imbolc. With each step in my discovery of her, I felt myself opening up to the gift of her presence in my life more and more.

Over the years that have followed, I have dedicated a lot of my fertility work with my clients to Brigid. She has continued to appear to me during periods of transition and difficulty. This Dark Night of The Soul was to bring another much-needed encounter with her and it was to happen as I gathered myself together for a podcast interview with two beautiful Goddesses from the Sense of Soul Podcast, Mande and Shanna.

As I logged into Zoom and Mande's video connected, up popped a background image of Brigid. Mande and I smiled as I told her that I took this as a beautiful sign that the Goddess was blessing our conversation. I knew that she was gifting me a message of new beginnings and trust. Her presence confirmed to me that I was slowly returning to myself.

I felt the wires reconnecting. The golden cords of light re-attaching and re-binding themselves to every part of me.

That conversation I had with Mande and Shanna reignited fully the flame within me that had been coughing and spluttering. Mande and Shanna had also begun to experience Brigid around them for the first time over recent weeks and so it was that we took her presence as a true blessing upon us that day.

Prayer of Connection to Brigid

If you feel called to connect with Brigid, here is a prayer of connection to the Goddess of New Beginnings. You can adapt and change the words if you feel called to. This connection prayer is simply what comes from my heart.

Place your hand over your heart and invoke the following words:

Beautiful Brigid,

Goddess of the Hearth of my heart,

Bringer of change

And new beginnings,

I invite you to connect with my spirit.

Re-connect me to my path,

Re-align my soul,

Lend me your fires of inspiration

And transformation.

Teach me to let go of the outcome,

To be present

With the pain and the joy.

To embrace the fertile shoots

Of new beginnings

Not yet known.

To trust the process,

To navigate this journey

With love and grace.

To honour the Maiden, Mother and Crone within.

To celebrate the Goddess

That I am blessed to be.

And so it is.

Thank you. Thank you.

Would you like to learn more about the different Gods, Goddesses and Pantheons? There is so much information out there. One of the modules that the members of my online magical community, *Natural Me Sisterhood* enjoy is on *Goddess/ Deity Study*.

If you are interested in learning more about the Sisterhood check out the links in the Connect with Me chapter towards the back of the book.

CTRIPLE GODDESS HEALING/ WELLNESS

In *Natural Magic for the Modern Goddess*, I share with you my concept of Triple Goddess Womb Healing – healing the Maiden, the Mother, and the Crone archetypes of our mind, body and spirit. I believe that in order to feel truly at one with ourselves and our Inner Goddess, we must embrace, love and heal the child, the adult and the grandmother/Crone that resides within us all.

As a therapist who specialises in women's health, I work a lot with the Triple Goddess archetypes in order to initiate Womb and Divine Feminine healing.

I want to dive deeper with you now, dear reader, into the psyche of the Triple Goddess that resides within you so that you may find wholeness, healing and love for the Goddess that you are. So that you may come to understand and respect how deeply entwined these three aspects of ourselves are with each other regardless of where we find ourselves to be in life, what age we are, and whether we feel happy and content in the present moment or not.

Nurturing a continued relationship with our Triple Goddess is a must, an ongoing love affair with our inner child, our mother aspect and our wise Crone self. You may think that the wisdom that comes with the Crone aspect can only be found when you physically enter into this phase of your life, but I will show you that this is absolutely not the case.

You may think that there is no wisdom to be found when connecting with your inner child, but oh my, how much do we underestimate the innate wisdom of our children?

You might perhaps, believe that where you find yourself to be right now, in the present is a place of struggle and lack of faith in yourself and your abilities to make the right choices in life. You may ask yourself, 'How can I make the right decisions when I don't trust myself and my judgement?' I promise you this, you hold the wisdom and all the answers to every question you have, within yourself. You just need to learn how to connect to and trust in your Inner Goddess intuition. I will show you how.

Let us take a look at the first archetype, the Maiden, and why, how and when we should connect with her.

THE MAIDEN

My belief is that we enter into the Goddess energy of each archetype for around 25-30 years before we move on to the next archetype in our Triple Goddess journey. However, that is not to say that we can't be under the embrace and influence of two archetypes at the same time. For example, you may still be on your Maiden journey when you become a mother. You will transition very quickly in every single way possible into your Mother archetype, but still be held within your Maiden phase of your life.

Your psyche, your body, your mind and spirit will evolve into the Mother with motherhood, but your body will also still be held within the youthful embrace of the Maiden, as perhaps your emotional development and maturity will too.

What a journey of transition to be in!

Our Maiden archetype is the dominant part of our soul that enters this world with us. She is with us when we take our first breath and transition through childhood and up to the age of 25.

The Maiden is pure, cosmic magic. She exudes an innocence about her that most perceive to come only from the naivety of childhood and a life that has barely lived.

However, what we perceive as innocence is in fact the pure white light of a soul that still remembers her origins before she entered this human existence. This innocence is the beauty of a soul that has yet to have the world and all its restrictions and negativity placed upon her. This innocence is the landscape of a lifetime laid out before her of endless possibilities and adventures. This innocence is the belief in herself that she is capable of anything and everything in this lifetime because she sees unquestionably her infinite potential in all things.

Her mind is free to imagine that she might one day be an astronaut, a marine biologist, a teacher, an actress, a wildlife conservationist. She remembers perhaps, more on a subconscious level that she came here with a mission to explore, to love and to light up the world with her very own, unique essence.

I think we have all come across a baby, toddler or young child of early primary school age that convinces us that they have been here before. They exude a wisdom and an understanding that we can only comprehend coming from a life that has already been lived. These little ones are often called 'old souls' and I for one have certainly witnessed elements of an old soul within both of my girls, especially as very young children. My belief is that this wisdom that they exude is a wisdom that is still remembered from a time when they were here on this planet before, a time when they lived a whole lifetime full of experiences that shaped their soul and played a part in its evolution into this current life.

I know what you are thinking as you are reading this. 'Where the heck did she go??'

I help my clients to connect to their Maiden Goddess when they are perhaps struggling with limiting beliefs, not-good-enoughs, or battling with reproductive problems or unexplained infertility. The emotional, psychological, energetic and physical blocks that are holding us back in life will come from an energetic blockage within our Maiden Goddess.

Perhaps at some point in our young life, we were emotionally imprinted upon by another in a negative way. The person responsible for this imprint may not have done so knowingly, but it is there, festering within our subconscious nonetheless. This negative imprint may have manifested from a major trauma or from an influence that chipped away upon our young Maiden Goddess, little by little over a prolonged period of time.

You may have witnessed a pattern of behaviour inflicted upon another person that has imprinted into your consciousness and is now impacting on the dynamics within your relationships with others as well as perhaps with yourself.

Ultimately, if you find yourself stuck in your current circumstances, trapped by fear and limiting beliefs and repeating the same negative patterns over and over again, some work needs to be done with your Maiden Goddess. This also includes health issues that have become chronic or keep returning time and again.

So, how do you go about beginning to connect with your Maiden Goddess in order to heal her shadows and bring about positive changes in your life, your circumstances and your health? Let us start with reconnecting that beautiful golden thread to her by reminding ourselves of who she was and is and continues to be.

Are you ready to embrace her and welcome her back with your arms and heart wide open? Let's do this!

MAIDEN MEDITATION

Find somewhere comfortable to sit down with your back straight and your eyes closed, somewhere you won't be disturbed. The place that you choose needs to feel safe so that you can allow any vulnerability to come to the surface.

I want you to imagine that you are standing in the middle of a beautiful summer meadow. The sun is shining and you can feel its warmth on your skin. As you gaze around you, hundreds of wildflowers are bobbing their heads amongst the long grass, caught on a soft summer breeze. You take a deep breath in through your nose and breathe in the scent of summer, of nature, of flowers, of fresh air.

Your feet are bare against the warm Earth below you, and you feel a deep, settled sense of contentment wash over you. In the distance, you notice someone walking through the meadow towards you. There is something familiar about her, in the way that she moves. As she draws closer and closer to you, you recognise her as yourself when you were a child.

She stops in front of you and smiles up at you, happy to see you again. You take in her features, her clothes, her expression.

How old does she/you appear to be? Think back to this time in your life. What was going on for you back then?

Were there any major changes or difficulties going on in your life?

What/who influenced you most at this time?

What were your dreams and aspirations?

Do you remember how you mostly felt at this time in your life?

Were you happy? Sad? Scared?

I want you to ask your Maiden-self to show you a time in your Maiden journey when something happened that would lead on to influence your life right up to the present day, something that you have struggled to deal with or process. Something that has created a negative impact on your life.

Allow the scene to unfold in your mind's eye, all the way to the very end. Remember, you are just the observer.

You are safe and nothing can hurt you.

When you reach the end of the scene, acknowledge how this memory has influenced and impacted on your young Maiden mind. View the situation from the perspective of your young, Maiden-self and how it made you feel when it happened.

Scan over your timeline between then and now and acknowledge the times when this shadow has held you back.

Now, I want you to imagine that you are back at the scene and I want you to place your hand over your heart and take some deep breaths in through your nose and out through your mouth.

Just breathe.

With every breath in I want you to imagine that you are filling up your lungs and your heart with a deep feeling of inner peace. As you imagine how this sense of peace makes you feel, you notice that it starts to evolve into a deep, heartfelt feeling of gratitude. Gratitude for the lesson that this situation has taught you and the resilience that it has given you.

Now view the situation through the eyes of your adult-self, from an adult perspective. See it for what it was back then and that, in fact, it was never about you, but about the other person. Or, was it a situation that simply occurred through the eyes of a child with a child's perspective? View the scene in your mind's eye as your adult-self with new clarity that has come with the wisdom of the life lessons that you have been gifted.

With every breath out, feel your body and your mind let go of the shadow, the negative energy, the child's perspective. Release it all and feel the lightness in your heart.

When you have sat with this beautiful feeling of lightness for a while, bring yourself back to the meadow and your Maiden-self stood in front of you. Ask her if she has a message for you and allow her words to fill your heart and mind.

Open your arms to her and wrap them around her. Cuddle her and love her with a fierceness that knows no bounds.

Wrap your arms around yourself now too.

She is you, and you are her.

Tell her that she is loved so very much. That she is brave and beautiful and deserving of so much love and happiness, that she can achieve anything that she sets her heart and mind to.

If you could give her one piece of advice, what would it be? Knowing what you know now?

Allow any tears to flow, any emotion to come to the surface and release. This is important for your healing to be successful.

When you are ready, let go of the little girl and look into her eyes, giving her silent thanks. Watch her slowly walk away through the meadow and gently open your eyes.

Give yourself a moment or two to just sit and reflect on your experience.

Whenever you feel old shadows and thoughts creeping back into your mind, remind yourself of the pact that you have made with your Maiden Goddess. Use the visualisation as often as needed.

Remember, your brain thrives on familiar routine and habitual thoughts and so you may find that it will want to return to the not-good-enoughs and negative talk from time to time. Stay vigilant and invite your Maiden Goddess in to support you.

Soul Questions

Grab your journal and write down the difference between how your adult-self witnessed the memory compared to how your child-self experienced it at the time.

What has been the biggest impact on your life since experiencing the situation that your inner-child showed you? In what ways have you perhaps felt held back?

What message did your inner child have for you?

How do you feel now you have finished the Maiden Meditation?

THE MOTHER

The Mother Goddess archetype resides predominantly within us from around the age of 25 to approximately 55-60 years old. In a similar way to the overlap that can happen between the Maiden and the Mother, so too can the Mother and the Crone archetype work alongside each other, but this time with both equally as strong and equally influential.

It is important to note that you do not have to become a parent in order to embody the Mother archetype. Equally, if you are in fact a parent and enter into the Crone archetype, your Mother energy will not diminish just because your kids have grown up. When you become a mother, you become one for life, not just for eighteen years of your child's life.

The Mother energy embodies a deep-rooted groundedness within her from the experiences of the road that she has travelled through life so far. While Maiden energy can be flighty and non-committal, the Mother has gained foresight and commitment to her course as well as a more conscious connection to herself and her needs. She is aware of what makes her tick and now feels relatively confident in her abilities as well as in her own skin, although this confidence can still hit its peaks and troughs as she commits.

It is within this phase predominantly that most women do the work on themselves in order to heal wounds and childhood shadows that are creating a negative impact on their present lives. Self-awareness and spiritual evolution have really hit their stride in the Mother Goddess phase of life.

A woman in her Mother Goddess archetype is the breaker of the chains that have bound her to situations and people that no longer lift her up, make her happy or fulfil her. The Mother

Goddess has gained a wisdom through hindsight that is a gift not only to herself but to others who lean on her for support. Women in the Mother archetype phase work closely with their Maiden energy in order to break karmic patterns of behaviour, get to the source of any unhappiness, and to strengthen their relationship and connection to themselves.

The woman who embodies her Inner Goddess is bold, fearless and confident in her abilities. She is a force to be reckoned with as her spirit unfolds within this period of her life, understanding that she is the keeper of her own destiny.

You will see with this archetype how working closely with the Maiden too is so often essential because her energy is entwined so deeply within the Mother. The need to heal and connect with the Inner Goddess archetype so often centres around the concept of self-love and acceptance. If a woman has struggled for most of her life with how she feels about herself, the first place that I always recommend that she begin her healing journey is by going back to connect to her Maiden. Once the work with the Maiden is done, it is then time to work within the present – the Mother Goddess that she is.

Life is usually so busy throughout this period of life, and our Inner Goddess's needs are often left at the bottom of a very big pile of to-dos that include work commitments, family and daily life. Creating time to l0ve, honour and nurture ourselves is seen as a luxury that time and inclination so often cannot afford. If Mother Goddesses aren't careful, burnout, stress and anxiety from overload will kick in and consistently knock her off her feet.

Connecting to your Inner Mother Goddess is imperative and is always in need of consistency when teaching yourself to know and accept from the bottom of your heart that you are worthy of feeling good and deserving of a place at the top of the pile.

Connecting to your Inner Mother Goddess is essential when nurturing a balance between your intuition and the wisdom and level-headedness that come with experience.

If you find yourself within the Mother archetype and struggling with your health and wellbeing, I can guarantee that you will find the root cause to be the lack of self-care and devotion to the needs of your mind, body and spirit. You will perhaps feel disconnected and a little lost at times throughout this period as you evolve and outgrow the old but are unsure of the new direction to take.

MOTHER MEDITATION

We are going to connect to the womb space of Gaia – Mother Earth – in this meditation, asking her to lend us her nurturing wisdom as Mother to all who call her Home. Gaia is the very embodiment of the Mother archetype as she feeds and nourishes us within the sacred and fertile landscape of her womb. When cherished and cared for, she flourishes, with those surrounding her flourishing alongside her. Gaia contains the magic of the elements and the wisdom of the cycles and seasons of her own nature. Connecting with her regularly will help you to connect to the wisdom that is reflected back to you within your own nature and season.

Get yourself comfortable with your back straight. If you are sat up, place your feet flat on the floor. Being outside for this meditation, perhaps with your back up against a tree, is even better but not essential.

Close your eyes and take some deep, cleansing breaths, in through your nose and out through your mouth. Allow your energy to settle down around your hips, or if you are lying down imagine that you are sinking into the sofa/bed with your energy gently settling to the back of your body.

Imagine that you are growing thick roots from the soles of your feet and from the base of your spine down into the Earth below you. Imagine how the Earth and soil feel as your roots push their way through the layers of Earth, rock, stones and bones, down deeper into Gaia past underground caverns and waterways.

Feel yourself anchoring fully into the surface/ground beneath you as you take strength from Mother Earth's hold on your body.

As you imagine your roots pushing deeper and deeper into the very heart of Gaia, they find their way into a beautiful, enormous cave made entirely of rose quartz. As your roots settle within the cave you take some deep breaths in through your nose and imagine that you are drawing that rosy, pink crystal energy up through your roots and straight into your body where it circulates and passes through every cell, every fibre, every organ and system. You can feel your body responding to this beautiful energy.

As you breathe out imagine that you are letting go of all tension from your body, allowing it to flow down into the Earth where it is neutralised and dispersed.

As you take note of this beautiful, enormous pink cavern, you walk slowly around the edge of the walls, running your fingers over the crystal, feeling the rough and the smooth and the exquisite energy of this gift from Gaia passing through your fingertips.

Make a note of any objects that you see within the room and any feelings that come up for you while you take in your surroundings. These are messages gifted to you from Gaia and your subconscious. There will be symbolism and meaning behind them.

At the very centre of the cavern is a deep pool carved into the rose quartz and filled with crystal-clear water that sparkles and shimmers as you move closer. This is Gaia's most sacred pool, containing all her nurturing love and wisdom that she has to offer you.

You remove your clothes and climb into the pool, enjoying the deliciousness of the cool water against your skin, revitalising your body and your mind. As you allow the water to hold you, you enjoy the feeling of weightlessness while you tune into your body. Have you been struggling with any aches and pains? Chronic conditions? Take a moment to consider when it was that you started to experience these discomforts. What was/ is going on in your life at the time? If you could attach a feeling to it, what would it be? Allow the heavy, uncomfortable feelings to pass through and out of your body with every breath out. Imagine the healing rose quartz water seeping deep into these places of discomfort, soothing, revitalising and restoring your body back to health.

Now ask the question, 'Where do I need to give myself more love and nurturing in my life and how can I do this? Gaia, Mother Earth, what do I need most right now?'

Enjoy the feeling of weightlessness, being held, nourished and restored back to a deeper more aligned sense of wellbeing as you float in the crystal pool.

When you feel ready, imagine that you are climbing out of the pool, dressing and returning to stand beneath the roots. As you prepare to be drawn up through the roots and back to your body you feel the weight of something in your right hand and notice that you are holding onto a beautiful piece of rose quartz, gifted to you by Gaia. You silently thank her for her love and support as you feel yourself being drawn back up through the roots, up, up through the layers of rock and soil, past caverns and waterways, past stones and bones and through the surface soil, the cool grass, the foundations of your house and back into your body. As you breathe in, you feel yourself settle fully back into your body.

You are safe and present. You have returned.

Slowly start to move your body, stretch and when you are ready, open your eyes and take a drink of water.

TASK

Open your journal and make a note of everything that you saw and felt during your journey into the heart of Gaia. What messages did you receive? Were there any objects in the cave? How do you feel now?

Write down what you feel that you need most right now and how you can take small steps to gift yourself this nourishment.

SOUL QUESTIONS

What insecurities have been cropping up for you recently or repetitively? Journal on where you think these insecurities come from and why. Do you need to re-visit your inner child?

As an extra bit of soul digging, think about how much you know now, the wisdom that has come from your journey so far, from the perceived mistakes and the hard lessons that you have learnt. Think about all the positives too. The love that you have experienced and the things that you hold most precious to your heart, feeling the gratitude for them all. Write down all these most precious of memories and experiences that have created the most impact in your life and shaped who you have become and the wisdom that you now carry within you. It's only when you look back that you realise how far you have come. Give yourself a big hug for being the incredible person that you are.

The Crone

As life and its lessons shape us, so too are we shaping and deepening the wise Crone energy that lies patiently within us, waiting for us to catch up and embrace the gifts of experience, a lifetime of lessons learnt and the hindsight that has come with it all. Most of all, the wise Crone within us is waiting for us to embrace the gratitude and acceptance for this wonderful life that we may never fully appreciate until the majority of it has passed us by, and there is more of it to look back on than there is road still left ahead of us.

The Crone is able to step out of the chaos of life and take on the role of observer as the pace of life slows a little, the reward for a lifetime of 'doing' is now the gift of time returned, time to devote to long-held desires that she could never justify investing the time or the money in, desires that focus only on filling moments, hours and days with creative endeavours, new adventures and time for connecting with nature and the little patch of the planet that she calls home.

The Crone will lose herself within the magical golden threads of time and space as she sinks her energy into trying new things or perhaps re-committing to life-long passions and projects that have fallen by the wayside over the course of her lifetime.

The guilt is removed. There is nowhere else she needs to be and no one else that needs her. She is free to choose how she spends her free time and she embraces and honours her right to do so as she settles into a whole new chapter of self-rediscovery that is much softer around the edges than with the first two Goddess chapters.

The Crone archetype comes to fruition between the age of 55-60 but as with the other two triple Goddess archetypes this isn't always definitive and can vary depending on what is still happening in a woman's life at this point. Most often though, a woman has transitioned or is transitioning through menopause and is perhaps starting to consider slowing down the pace of life, whether it means reducing working hours or considering retirement in the next handful of years.

If she has borne children in her lifetime, they will have grown up and settled into their own lives, no longer commanding her time as they did when they were younger and still needing guidance from their mother. The wise Crone energy does not arrive solely after parenthood. The wise Crone resides within every woman entering these years of her life, born from a lifetime of experience and wisdom gathering.

As I mentioned earlier, there is an overlap with the archetypes, but I believe that there is none more so prevalent than between the Maiden and the Crone. In fact, I feel it is less of an overlap and more a weaving of the two energies that can be witnessed most strongly within the first 5-10 years after entering the Crone phase, similar to the energy of the first 5 years of childhood. The daily grind and the burden of juggling life, family, finances and time are falling away and the Crone is remembering what it feels like to commit only to fun and what lights her soul on fire. The last time that she had this outlook on life was more than likely in childhood before she was taken over with responsibilities and commitments. So often the Crone will find that she nurtures a more playful and easygoing connection with her grandchildren than she had time for with her own, understanding that time is precious and it passes too quickly. She knows that creating a time of play and fun with the younger generation is of utmost importance, especially because she realises just how serious life can become as we get older and leave our childhood behind.

Connecting to the wise Crone energy within us at whichever phase of our life we find ourselves to be in really can be simpler than we think.

When you are struggling to find the answers in life, often feeling lost and directionless and desperate for some guidance and wisdom, simply turn inwards and imagine your wise Crone-self sat in her favourite armchair having lived a full life with no regrets, only lessons learnt and wise stories to be told. If you were her, looking back on your life and being asked for advice, what would it be? Come from a place of impartiality. Come from a place of acceptance that life is about making choices that feel right at the time. There is no right or wrong.

What advice would you give your grandchildren if they asked you the same question that you are seeking the answer to? Imagine the answer that you would offer if your heart wasn't as invested as it may be right now. Imagine the answer that you would offer if time or money or worrying about pleasing other people were not on the agenda. What advice would you offer, coming from the person who had lived more of her life than what may remain of the future ahead of her, understanding that life is fleeting, and every moment is precious?

This is where your wise Crone Goddess resides.

CRONE MEDITATION

Get yourself comfortable in a spot where you won't be disturbed, and close your eyes. You may wish to sit outside if the weather is warm and sunny, perhaps with your back up against your favourite tree.

Imagine strong roots growing out of the soles of your feet and the base of your spine, down into the Earth below you, settling deep within Mother Earth and holding you firm and grounded to her surface.

Take a deep breath in through your nose for four seconds, and out through your mouth for four seconds. Repeat this a few times until you feel calm and settled, your energy sitting heavy and weighted around your hips.

In your mind's eye, imagine that you are nestled within a deep green and luscious forest. You are in fact one of the beautiful and magnificent trees. You can feel your ancient roots nestled deep within the Earth and you can feel the soft, warm breeze rustling the green leaves along your long, elegant branches.

Your energy is woven throughout the tree, which you discover is an oak tree as you study the leaves more closely. The oak tree is renowned for her wisdom and deep inner strength amongst all trees, and you are a part of this tree and yet you are also separate from it.

As you enjoy the sunshine and the soft breeze and the nourishment from Mother Earth below you, you close your eyes and breathe into the deep well of ancient wisdom that resides within you from a lifetime of weathering every storm that you have ever faced, every foggy unknown that has ever enveloped itself around you, every lesson that has seemed almost impossible to comprehend at the time.

Here, within this moment, you can stand still and witness life unfolding around you. You are the observer and yet you are still very much a part of it all.

You notice after a while two figures walking towards you in the distance. As they draw closer you can see that one is a young child and the other is a woman, perhaps in her thirties or forties. You look into their faces and recognise that they are you. Your Maiden-self and your Mother-self from what seems like so long ago now.

As they approach the base of your trunk and look up into your branches you notice that there is a little remembrance plaque attached to the bark which has your name on it with a message of love from your family. You passed into spirit some time ago and this place is where your soul often drifts to when you are remembered with love.

Your Maiden and your Mother Inner Goddesses are seeking your wisdom at this time as with something that they may be struggling to find the answer to right now. They are calling upon your spirit to guide them and as they do, you feel yourself gently separate your energy from the ancient oak tree and stand before them in beautiful, rich green robes, your hair falling wildly around your shoulders.

You look into their eyes and can see your life unfolding within your memory as if you have once again become the observer of yourself. You watch many different memories unfold and witness how you dealt with them all at the time. Some you handled really well, others not so much.

Your Maiden and Mother-self show you a vision of something that they are struggling with, and you watch it unfold within the reflection of their eyes. You observe without judgement, without attachment or emotion and you see with clarity the solution that has evaded your younger self until now.

You share your knowledge with them and they thank you for your guidance and strength as you wrap your arms around them both and remind them that the answers they seek will always be found within themselves, they just have to trust their intuition and their instinct.

As they turn back towards the direction from which they came you feel your spirit melt back into the oak and transform into pure energy that drifts up through the leaves and out into the heavens.

Enjoy this sense of one-ness and freedom for a moment before bringing your awareness back into your body, within this present moment of time and space.

Take some deep breaths in and out and gently start to wiggle your fingers and toes. Grab yourself a glass of water and take your journal out while the memory of your journey is still fresh in your mind.

SOUL QUESTIONS

What memory or situation did your Maiden or Mother-self want your guidance with?

What message did your wise Crone Goddess have for them? Consider your thoughts on the clarity that you experienced when you stepped back and changed your perspective from being in the thick of the situation that you were experiencing to the observer who just sat and silently witnessed with a broadened and more detached perspective.

Sometimes we need to step back outside of our own headspace when we are struggling to understand or find clarity on a situation and witness the bigger picture rather than get lost in the emotion of it all which can often cause us to lose our sense of balanced perspective.

Always come back to your wise Inner Crone and ask her what she would do, purely as an observer.

HEAL - SUMMARY & REFLECTIONS

We have journeyed deep into the past with this Pillar, understanding our shadows and where they come from, be they from this lifetime or a past lifetime. We have acknowledged them and we have re-framed them. We have created a beautiful healing ritual to honour and heal our womb and reproductive space, facing the ancient truths that connect us to our lineage and past lives. We have journeyed through the darkness in order to return to the light and with it we have met my patron Goddess, Brigid, and possibly explored other ancient deities that we feel drawn to work with along the way as part of our healing journey.

We have re-familiarised ourselves with the Triple Goddess, this time travelling into the psyche of the Maiden, Mother and Crone who reside within us all in order to heal our Maiden-self, our Mother-self and our Crone-self.

Here are some soul questions for you now that we have worked deeply within our Heal Goddess Pillar.

SOUL QUESTIONS

How can becoming the observer in a difficult or painful situation give you strength?

Since working through the Shadow Work sections, do you feel like you have released your shadows? Explain how you feel.

Do you think you may have to return to the Re-frame Your Shadows meditation if needed?

When you did the Reproductive Massage and Womb Healing Ritual, did you experience memories or emotions that you were not expecting? Explain your answer.

Do you feel drawn to learning about a particular ancient God or Goddess? Write down some facts and information here that you have discovered so far.

PILLAR FOUR

LOVE

As we move onto our next Pillar of Goddess – Love – it is important to recognise that we can in fact still be within the Heal Pillar while we move through the Love Pillar. When I talk about love in this Pillar, we learn to nurture and harness love for ourselves first and foremost before we explore the concept of Soul Contracts within relationships as well as finding a balance between the Divine Feminine and Divine Masculine.

For most of us journeying through our Heal Pillar, we are so focused on our inner journey with ourselves that we are taken by surprise when someone enters our life and we strike up a connection that we were not expecting, let alone think that we are ready for. And yet, our heart wants what it wants and the inexplicable pull towards love with another is possibly the most magnetic pull we will ever experience.

So, how do we continue to honour the healing of our Inner Goddess while stepping into the Love Pillar, whether we are ready for it or not? How do we learn to love and cherish ourselves as well as another while attempting to not make the same mistakes again that may lead to heartache?

How do we keep our Inner Goddess at the top of her Pillar without getting lost within the foggy breathlessness of a new love?

Now that we have worked so hard on our journey with our self and our Inner Goddess, we must learn to recognise the red flags if they arise and act upon them. We may not have always done so in the past – it might have felt easier to ignore the little niggles initially that eventually became a tidal wave that we couldn't ignore.

Love holds the highest energetic frequency there is, and although to love can be the most freeing thing to do, everything in life requires balance in order to thrive. We want our Inner Goddess to thrive, so let's take a look at how we can navigate this beautiful Pillar with ourselves and with others.

KEEPER

You are the keeper of something sacred, the embodiment of physical light. You are the earthly anchor to something eternal, the part of you that shines bright.

You are the temple of sacred truths, the personification of light and love.

You committed to connect completely to below you, and above.

Your mission each time that you return is to trust and to live your truth, to weave the magic that you were gifted, commitment is the only proof,

that your mission sings within your heart is the reason you came to be, the reason you chose to breathe again, the reason you chose to see.

Remember the miracle of who you are, the uniqueness that shines within your soul has been crafted for lifetimes, always ready to begin, another journey, a lesson, a life, a goal, each breath a wondrous gift.

For you are the keeper of your soul.

Let your soul and spirit lift!

YOUR GODDESS PHILOSOPHY

The idea of creating your very own unique and personal Goddess philosophy is that you use it as a daily, positive mantra. Think of it as a huge neon flashing signpost that helps to keep you on track every day, and helps to point you in the right direction when you are feeling lost and directionless.

It might be that you have read a philosophy or mantra elsewhere that really resonates with you, so feel free to adopt it as your own. I often believe that when we take the time to create our own philosophy, we gift ourselves the magic of really tapping into our intuition, our Inner Goddess, and stepping back for a moment to allow her voice to shine through and be heard over the everyday noise.

If you had a few words that could sum up what you believe your life should be all about, what would it be?

Imagine your 85-year-old Grandmother-you being asked for her philosophy on life. What would she say? What would she believe was truly important after spending a lifetime on this Earth?

If she looked back on her life, what do you think her most precious memories and gifts would be?

Make a list of everything that you believe to be so very sacred and fundamental to living your life to the full, with no regrets or sadness for the things you should have done.

What do you believe to be the cornerstones of a happy and well-lived life? Write them down and arrange them into your very own personal philosophy. For example, the cornerstones for your happy life might be contentment, freedom, love and health. Your philosophy might read something like this:

I find contentment and happiness when I love without restriction, nourish my body and allow myself the freedom to be who I truly am.

Now place your philosophy somewhere that you can read it every day. Your philosophy will help to keep you connected to your Inner Goddess. It will remind you that you are in exactly the right place at the right time when there are times you feel like you are questioning everything.

Your philosophy will be your beam of torchlight that guides you through the darkness when you are feeling lost.

Your philosophy and the energy behind it will grant you direct access to the higher realms of consciousness, to spirit, to your guides and to the Universal Law of Attraction.

Watch how quickly your days begin to unfold with more grace and flow.

Boundaries & saying no

When we initiate ourselves fully into being the Goddess that we came here to be, one of the first things that we must do is take a long, hard look at the personal boundaries that we have created and currently have in place in our life. These boundaries are potent and so very important to the survival and thrival of our spirit. If our boundaries are not in place, or are perhaps overlooked, then we are not looking after ourselves and honouring ourselves for the Goddess that we are.

Do you feel that your boundaries are solid and indestructible? Or, do they feel invisible or so weak that they might blow away in a light breeze?

A strong Goddess with strong Goddess energy reflects upon and nurtures her boundaries daily. These invisible barriers are protective for our soul, body and spirit. Sometimes, you may find that they move and adjust with the flow of your life and the experiences you have. These boundaries are perhaps peripheral and ever-changing, but others may have been built a long time ago. They may even have been placed there from another lifetime. These boundaries are non-negotiable, immovable forces of protection and you honour them unequivocally.

Let's take a look, first of all, at the boundaries that every Goddess should have in place for the survival and thrival of her Inner Goddess – these are non-negotiable and immovable.

You are:

- Able to say no when something does not feel right and your intuition is telling you NO, without fear or guilt.

- Loving yourself and honouring your needs before all others.

- Holding your happiness and health in the very highest regard.

- Always honouring what feels good to you and what lights you up.

- Surrounding yourself only with those that lift you up and make you feel good.

- Allowing what doesn't feel good and is no longer aligned to fall away with love, grace and gratitude.

- Respecting and cherishing your mind, body and spirit above any other/all else.

- Never allowing the negative thoughts and opinions of others to permeate and convince you that you are in any way less than, not good enough, or unworthy of unconditional love.

- Not allowing others more than a second chance to hurt you and break your heart.

These boundaries are the ones that you will more than likely struggle with throughout your lifetime. As you read them, I can feel the energy of your mind as you nod in acknowledgment. I occasionally struggle with some of them too.

Many life lessons come with the strength and bond that we

have to these boundaries. We will find that they are not always easy to uphold or maintain for fear, mostly, of repercussions from others, but ultimately because we balance our love for ourselves on a knife edge, forgetting to hold ourselves in the highest regard in all matters, in all situations and with all people.

It is always so much easier for so many of us to honour others' needs and wishes before and above our own. For many of us, the need to feel loved and accepted overshadows all things. In these moments, deep down your Inner Goddess is desperately shouting her lungs out at you to be heard and to remind you to honour yourself, but you drown her out – a practice that you have become so good at over the years as you ignore the call from Her.

As a society, we create laws, boundaries that are simply not crossed. If you break them, there are consequences. For the most part, many of these laws are built on the foundations of what we know to be unequivocally true – the difference between an act that is right and one that is wrong. We know and feel these 'rights' and 'wrongs' on a deep, cellular level. There is never any question around them, no arguing or suggesting that the boundaries be blurred in certain circumstances, in any way, shape or form. We know that rape is rape for example. We know that to take the life of another human being intentionally is wrong.

Take a minute to ponder over these laws and any others you may think of, not just considering them as a law but how you feel on a moral level, from a spiritual and emotional perspective.

Every fibre of your being goes against these acts of violence. You may feel repulsed, anguish, a deep sadness for those who experience these darkest of acts carried out by other human beings. You may experience or have experienced a fear that you might one day find yourself in one of these situations.

The point that I am trying to make is that there are some boundaries that we simply do not cross. There is no question surrounding their validity. The strong sense of right and wrong that you feel should now be applied with utter solidity to the non-negotiable Goddess Boundaries. Not to compare to these monstrous and terrible acts, but to lend you a sense of energetic perspective when it comes to how powerfully and solidly you uphold them for your very sense of self-preservation.

These boundaries need to be held with the same conviction as you do the solid belief between right and wrong. These non-negotiable boundaries need a cut-and-dry approach, a 'this is how it is – period' mindset.

So, how do you solidify your non-negotiable boundaries into your psyche, trusting that they will stand the test of time and anyone who tries to breach them, namely yourself?

Take a look back at the list and circle the ones that you uphold in every situation. Use a green pen or pencil. Now circle the ones that you struggle with, that perhaps you find inconsistent in your life, your friendships, relationships with work colleagues – every area of your life. You can circle these in red pen or pencil if you like.

Now take your journal, a piece of paper or some post-it notes and write out the red boundaries, in a list if you are writing in your journal or a piece of paper. If you are using post-its, you can write each one on an individual post-it. Place your post-its/ paper or journal somewhere that you can read them every day. This way, your boundaries are being woven gently into your subconscious daily until they create deep, immovable roots within your mind. Over time, the words and the energy that they carry with them will take a firm hold and you will feel them settle within your psyche.

Our minds work best at retaining knowledge and energy when there is a routine, a constant approach to the way that we do things. The more that we train our brain and our mind to think a certain way, the stronger its retention will become – but slack off and quit the exercise and it all turns to mush. We can all relate to that, right?

Now that we have established our non-negotiable boundaries, let's define the peripheral boundaries. These boundaries are fluid and adaptable in their approach to situations. They will shift as you move through life and your soul continues to grow and re-establish its strength and its path with each new experience and life lesson.

Your peripheral boundaries are a little like the subtle differences that you find in your friendships. Each of your friends are different and unique, which means that your friendship is like no other. The dynamics between yourself and each individual friend are tailored to your personalities and how you connect with each other in a harmonious way.

You may have one friend for example, who is notoriously rubbish at replying to messages, but you have learnt not to take it personally because that is just how they are, consistently inconsistent with everyone.

However, one of your other friends is always punctual with her replies and her communication but decides over the course of a few days or weeks that she can't be bothered to reply to your messages. You, of course, will find this behaviour unacceptable and out of character. You may worry or get angry and frustrated. You will find it hard to let this neglect slide without a solid justification. A friend is a friend, right?

But, each friendship is different therefore boundaries are different. As you move through life and experience the changes that it brings, you will always find yourself re-assessing your peripheral boundaries in order to tailor them to your current circumstances. This is part of life, adapting and growing into each new circumstance, situation or relationship.

Take a moment to think about the jobs that you have had over the years. Each one comes with its own job specification and the hours that you are meant to work in order to uphold your end of the contract and get paid. If you had a 20-hour-a-week contracted employment you would find it unacceptable if you were made to feel that you were expected to work double the hours without notice or the pay. If, however, you take on a zero-hour contract then you accept that you have to have some flexibility when you are asked to work short notice. You will make yourself available for the work because you won't know how long it will be until you are asked to work again. You accept that life will be a little unpredictable.

The boundaries with each job are individual, separate and unique. The same applies to your relationships and each of your circumstances. You may think back to a relationship you had in which you had to adapt to that person who worked long hours and therefore struggled to nurture a work/life balance with you. The relationship broke down and when you eventually thought about what you wanted from a new relationship, you realised that being with someone who could offer you more of their time and more consistency was much more important to you than you realised before the start of your last relationship.

Fill out the following charts and consider each area of your life for a moment and where you hold peripheral and non-negotiable boundaries from past experiences and present circumstances. I have added some examples for you to begin with.

Past Boundaries

HOME		WORK		RELATIONSHIPS	
Non-neg.	periph.	Non-neg.	periph.	Non-neg.	periph.
Safe space	Location	Work to paid hours	Work later if needed	Do not cheat	Reply to my messges promptly

Present Boundaries

HOME		WORK		RELATIONSHIPS	
Non-neg.	periph.	Non-neg.	periph.	Non-neg.	periph.
Safe space	House over location	Work to paid hours	Offer extra hours	Do not cheat	Reply to messages dependant on necessity when you can

GODDESS BOUNDARIES INVOCATION

'I am the protector of this Goddess,
In mind, body and spirit.
I hold her close
And honour her wishes.
As she unfolds, life unfolds,
Magic unfolds.
My boundaries are strong, firm
Withstanding every hurt, every pain,
Every attempted breach.
For my Inner Goddess
Is the most sacred part of me,
To be honoured, heard
And loved unconditionally.
My boundaries are my guide,
The gatekeepers to my soul
And I will always
Honour and protect them.
I will always remind myself of their presence

And give thanks for the strength they offer me.

My boundaries sparkle

Like gold,

Gifted and adorned

In my most favourite of flowers,

A symbol of the love and respect

That I give myself

With every breath I take.

And so it is!'

HONOURING YOUR INNER GODDESS IN YOUR RELATIONSHIPS

Imagine devoting your time, your energy, your love, your soul, to cherishing and adoring your Inner Goddess, understanding her needs, her desires and committing to finally, for the first time in your life, putting her first, at the very top of the pile. Lifted so high and enjoying her lofty throne in her temple in the sky.

You have done the work and you continue to do the work every single day, until the day someone walks into your life completely unexpected, certainly un-asked for because you have been too busy adoring yourself.

But oh, what a gift this person is to your life. A gift that leaves your head spinning, your thoughts muddled, your tummy consistently fluttering and your heart skipping a beat.

All of a sudden, just like that, your Inner Goddess topples from her throne and disappears in a puff of smoke, never to be worshipped again.

Why do we find it so easy to let our Inner Goddess fall when our focus is turned towards another? What impact does this really have on our relationships as we continue to lay the foundations in our new relationship?

How can we spot the warning signs and save not just the health and vitality of our fledgling relationship, but our first and truest love, our Inner Goddess?

Those who have read my first book will be familiar with my personal journey of self-discovery. You will know how long it took for me to finally acknowledge my Inner Goddess and put her on top – a place that she had never been before.

It took a decade of deep soul searching, my soul cracking open twice, and the birth of my first book, to finally arrive here within me, fully integrated and owning my Inner Goddess for all that she is worth.

With the birth of my book, the final shadows fell away and my marriage along with it. Deep down I always knew that it was going to happen this way, but I was more than ready to step into this new chapter of my life as a single and independent woman, pledging allegiance to the next decade of my life to be all about me, myself and I.

My forties were going to be the first-ever chapter of my life that didn't focus on having a man in it in order to feel that my life had meaning and purpose.

I didn't need to look for love from another in order to feel loved because I now fully understood and honoured what it meant to love myself.

Until the day my head was turned, and my world spun on its axis.

A few short months after my marriage ended, a man from my past re-entered my life in a completely unexpected way. We only connected for five months in total, but what those five months brought to my life was an explosive mix of casual, intense, hit-and-miss communication, intense desire and a ton of anxiety.

'B' and I lived nowhere near each other, his work schedule was insane and his precious little free time was spent with his little boy. We struggled to create any time to see each other and yet we connected almost daily, depending on whereabouts in the world he was.

With each day that passed, the energetic cord between us got stronger and I became more frustrated at our inability to really get this potential relationship off the ground. B's communication was hit and miss at the best of times, but when you threw into the mix his travelling schedule, the inconsistency that I experienced with him left me feeling insecure, always questioning and unable to focus on anything else. I had never had to chase someone for their attention before, but I felt like I was turning into the one pursuing rather than experiencing a mutual and balanced connection with someone.

Despite the uncertainties and the insecurities that surfaced regularly with B, I felt like I was still being pulled inexplicably towards him and he to me. I felt a lot of frustration from both of us regarding his chaotic work life which impacted so heavily on him being unable to sustain a personal life.

As I look back on those months with him in my life, I realise that this time with him contributed to the major lows that I had started to experience after reconnecting with him. When I left my marriage, it was hard, yes, painfully excruciating, yes, however, there was a solid foundation of belief and trust underneath it all that I had finally made the decision that I had been avoiding for so long. This is what held me anchored and steadfast on my path ahead of me, despite the unknowns. When B entered my life, however, I began to wobble majorly on my foundations. The anxiety was like nothing that I had ever experienced in my life. I lost my appetite for two months and the weight began to fall from my body. Do I believe that it may in part have been a delayed reaction to my separation? Of course, but I also believe that, deep down, I knew that I was losing control of my Inner Goddess and her values, wishes and boundaries. I was beginning to repeat the same mistakes, creating the same negative patterns in my life and relationships that I had become so painfully aware of halfway through my marriage. And yet, here I was, all the wiser and yet continuing to fall into the same traps that I set up for myself over and over again.

The day that I finally let go of B and moved on from him, I had spent the majority of that day walking in one of my favourite places in nature, a place where I could hear the whispers of my Inner Goddess the strongest. A place where I could hear the wisdom and guidance from my main spiritual guide, Karim. I had ignored them both for too long and I was finally ready to listen, tune in and place my Inner Goddess back on her throne.

As I walked and pondered on why on Earth the Universe would bring me so much inner turmoil and conflict on top of everything else that I was trying to navigate my way through, I realised that the Universe had given me exactly what I had asked for. In fact, I had reaffirmed over and over again in conversations with friends as well as within my own thoughts that I wanted a man who didn't want commitment on a full-time basis, who just wanted fun as and when it suited, who might whisk me away occasionally for a weekend of fun and adventure. The mixed messages that I was giving the Universe were so confusing.

Despite wanting this relationship to go somewhere with B, the undercurrent of energetic thoughts was that I didn't want and wasn't ready for a relationship. I knew this more than anything, and yet I tried to ignore what my heart knew because this connection had lit a spark in me that I hadn't felt in such a long time, so much so that all other sense of rhyme or reason went out the window.

The debilitating anxiety that I had been experiencing was coming from the knowledge deep down that I didn't really want this relationship, but my ego was in a fight with my Inner Goddess, trying to prove something to itself, that I was still desired and wanted as a single woman approaching 40.

After everything that I knew and understood about cultivating love within in order to feel love with-out, I was still finding myself repeating the same mistakes.

As I cut the energetic cords with B and started to move forward with my life once more, I still felt like I was sinking deeper into a deep, dark pit of despair. Christmas was approaching, the house had sold and I knew that, come the new year, I needed to find myself and my girls somewhere to live, somewhere that wouldn't make me feel as if I had failed them more than I felt I already had by ripping their family apart and forcing them to move from the only home that they knew to somewhere that was inevitably going to be 'less than' in every single way.

My ego was embroiled in a raging battle with my heart and all that I knew to be true about the decision that I had made to leave my husband, my girls' father.

As January 2022 arrived, wet, cold and miserable, kicking at the heels of Christmas the panic set in as I searched with misery for a new home for the girls and me.

I had made my peace with the fact that I needed to rent for at least a year while my work got back onto an even keel after the disruption from Covid, but I was not prepared for the hell that I was thrown into when trying to find somewhere that would not only allow me to use my home for business purposes but was decent enough to call a home without a ridiculous rental price attached to it.

I also realised that where I needed to rent, houses were few and far between and came at a premium. Because of this, people would actually sit and refresh their search feed throughout the day, waiting to be the first to snap up the next property that came up like gold dust. I had no chance of getting a look-in. I worked days and evenings which meant that by the time I sat down to take a look at anything half-decent, it was already gone.

As I began to despair at the bleak outlook of my circumstances I also prayed to the Universe with very specific details on my perfect 'stop-gap' house finding me at the right time and told myself daily that everything was as it should be.

A few short days after finding a private landlord who had a property coming onto the market in a couple of months, I contemplated the fact that I was prepared to pay way over my budget for rent in order to secure my peace of mind that I would have a new and freshly refurbished home for myself and my girls, despite the rent of nearly £1000 a month making me feel uncomfortable, when my phone rang. It was my friend Craig who managed a local property rental company and he had something to show me that he thought would tick all the boxes. As he walked me round the house on his phone screen I could have cried with relief. Not only had he found me a beautiful little house, it was in the perfect location, it was newly decorated and had the perfect price attached to it for rent.

Moving into this house, despite the fact that I did not own it, was the freedom that I had so desperately been craving for, longer than I care to recall.

Living in our marital home for nine months after separating was the very worst kind of limbo and came with very few boundaries between my husband and me. You know that whole chapter that I wrote earlier on the importance of boundaries? Yep, well, even after ending my marriage I still found myself struggling to maintain my own boundaries because I felt I didn't deserve to have them. This was the guilt talking (and others) because I believed that I had taken enough, too much as it was from myself, my husband and my girls. Yet again I was in a place that meant that I had honoured what I truly felt and made the hardest decision that I have ever had to make, but still felt unworthy of honouring my boundaries for what was to come in the aftermath of it all.

This house was confirmation of my biggest boundary that I had finally established, and it felt good to shut my own front door. It felt good to be able to breathe again within my own space and most importantly, after nearly a year of separation but not actually feeling fully separated, I felt free to move on with my life, in my own way. To be able to make plans for the future, find some normality again for the girls as well as myself. Most of all, to really be able to settle into this new period of my life within the privacy of my own home meant that I could finally close old wounds and heal in a peaceful space that only held the bright threads of the future within it.

As life moved swiftly forward, so too did everything else around me. Work became super busy once more now that the Universe could feel that I was ready and energetically available to get going again, and plans for holidays to some of our favourite places were well underway as spring passed by in the blink of an eye, bowling us towards the warm and much-anticipated return of the long summer months ahead.

On the day of my 40th solar return, I began my journey into a two-year Goddess Astrology training that I had felt drawn towards for such a long time, as well as secured my place on the next shamanic womb healing course in September.

I had also bitten the bullet and found myself the most wonderfully gifted of virtual assistants to finally help support my work with Natural Me, and I was finally back in my zone of magic with my work and my purpose.

I felt energised, aligned, on fire with creative ideas, and I felt relieved more than anything else that my passion for my work had returned. For a moment there as I wandered blindly through the darkness, I wasn't sure if I would ever want to return to what I do.

As the months rolled by the topic of dating began to crop up amongst conversations with my friends. Although I hadn't really had the time or the headspace to give it much thought, I could feel something gently starting to unfurl from around my heart once more and the thought of connecting with someone was a thought that I didn't shy away from as much as I thought that I would.

I still wasn't looking for any kind of major commitment, perhaps something gentle, slow and easygoing was what I needed. The trouble is that I have never been built for 'casual'. I'm either all-in or not at all and for that reason I had chosen to keep myself away from anybody or any situation that might lend itself the opportunity for me to meet someone that I wasn't ready to commit to. I didn't want to repeat what happened with B and to be honest, at that point I still felt a lot of confusion about what it was that I did actually want from another person, if anything at all right now.

Despite all the question marks, however, I put a silent prayer out to the Universe to send me someone who was gentle, kind, interesting, funny, passionate, attentive but gave me my freedom, didn't smother me, had his own life to lead but was committed to me nonetheless.

Two weeks later another person from my past re-entered my life and this time completely bowled me over. We connected in a way that held so much history between us as friends but also in the delicious way that new lovers create fiery sparks together as something new ignites for the first time between them.

We began re-connecting in a gentle way to begin with as we rediscovered one another and caught up on the 24+ years since we had last seen each other, but very quickly things progressed, and we were sharing our thoughts and feelings with each other with mutual amazement at how life had brought us back together in such an unexpected and unforeseen way.

Logistics was an issue, however. He lived four hours away and I was already beginning to wonder how this would work. He had family commitments with his children, as I had with my own, and very soon the niggle began to return in the undercurrent of what flowed so easily between us. It was a mere three short weeks before I simply couldn't ignore it anymore. I couldn't allow another five months of my life to pass me by as I slowly sank into a deep pit of despair once more. It had taken every part of me to drag myself out of it and to get to where I was now. I could not, I would not put myself through that again.

With a heavy heart, I called time on what I knew could have been something truly beautiful, if only our circumstances had been different. The night I said goodbye to C, I felt a familiar, deep ache settle within my heart.

Despite honouring my intuition and my Inner Goddess and listening to the niggle much sooner this time, I still wondered what bloody game the Universe and I had going on that I was not privy to. Why had I been gifted yet another man who ultimately was not available? And why bring him to me when I was still not quite out of the woods with my emotional instability?

As I lay wretchedly for hours in the darkness, trying to hold back the tears so as not to disturb my girls, it was then that I realised that I had, once again, given the Universe a mixed bag of signals.

I also realised that I needed to find acceptance in what love meant to me and what it was that I truly needed instead of still trying to keep one foot in and one foot out as a way of trying to control how much love I gave a person.

My fear of love had been born from relationships, including friendships, that always started out as something beautiful but ended with me walking away because I'd grown tired of feeling smothered and emotionally manipulated by another. My experiences with any kind of relationship were that the person I gave my heart to would always end up taking more and more, the boundaries blurring between us as I found it hard to maintain respect and boundaries for what it was that I needed from fear of offending the other person, regardless of how they were making me feel. I was fully endorsing that my wants and needs and happiness were to always come below someone else's and because of my inability to maintain personal boundaries, I found it easier to walk into relationships at arm's length, making it easier to leave as inevitably I would, every single time.

So here it was that I found myself, finally understanding that the reason I was continuing to attract unavailable people into my life was because I was asking the Universe to find me someone who ultimately was not fully available to commit to me –because I wasn't ready to commit either.

Love knows no half-measures, only whole truths of what lies at the very centre of a person's heart.

Love is the fullest and highest energetic expression of all others, and it cannot be tamed, only embraced with a full and open heart that is ready to receive it all, the good, the not so good and everything in between.

When your Inner Goddess is shining bright with love for yourself, your heart wide open to receiving love from yourself and love from another, only then will you find the people that will share with you a whole and pure love that mirrors what already lies within you.

Our energy is magnetic. Like attracts like. It is the Law of Attraction and there is no escaping or hiding from it. There is no convincing the Universe of your half-truths when it comes to love, beautiful Goddess. Only one question ever needs to pass through your mind and heart – do you fully embrace the love that you have for yourself, accepting and honouring that you are deserving of a full and unconditional love from within in order to receive it fully from another?

If you think, love, honour and adore your Inner Goddess, you will be loved, honoured and adored in return by others.

You must know and understand fully that your life is your own, and so is your identity. You came here to be you and as an added gift, to then enjoy the union that takes place when you love another, unconditionally, without restraints placed upon you both, but free to choose one another. This is love. This is why it is so important to always love and honour your Inner Goddess above all others. This is how you will find union not only within yourself but with your lovers, your partners, your soul mates.

Allow yourself to be your fullest expression of love.

SOUL QUESTIONS

Think about a significant relationship, either current or past and the dynamic of it that you struggled with in particular. Consider how well you honoured your Inner Goddess at the time. Was she at the top of the Pillar? Explain your experience.

Have you noticed that you have experienced the same or similar dynamic in more than one of your relationships? Where do you see the pattern of behaviour that links to the strength of your relationship with your Inner Goddess?

Have you always found it easy to honour your Inner Goddess in your relationships? If not, consider why you might have struggled. Where do you think the root of this struggle may have come from?

When have you convinced yourself that you wanted something when in fact, deep down, the truth is that you wanted the opposite?

Think about one way that you would choose to honour your Inner Goddess from now on. What would it be?

WHEN YOU ARE READY

It's not the same doing it all over again – love, that is – when you have lived a life that comes with stories, history that is painful, a heart that has been shattered and put back together again and children that might be a very deep consideration with the choices that you make.

From my own experience, at 41 years old I think more, worry more. I'm set in my ways, and there is a fear of opening up my heart again.

And yet...

I am stronger, I know what I want and what I won't put up with. I have the deepest understanding of how far down I can fall when it falls to pieces, but I also know how far I can rise up again more resilient and open to love than ever before. Perhaps this will resonate with your Inner Goddess story too?

Be determined to keep your heart open despite moments of absolute fear and darkness that attempt to close it off. Continue to nurture your relationship with yourself, understand and listen to yourself with a trust that is unrivalled to any other time in your life because, at the end of everything, it is only you that can pull yourself up again.

It is not easy to love again, but despite moments of panic that you will likely experience because you can feel yourself falling and there is nothing you can do to stop it, the kind of love that comes with life and history and past stories will be deeper and more magnetic that anything that has come before.

The best part of being human is to love.

There is no one worth closing your heart off for.

MY SOUL RECOGNISED YOU

My soul recognised you
Before my eyes did.
My heart beat faster
In remembering you.
Two souls returning,
Spheres colliding,
Absorbing, re-discovering.
A sense of familiarity
Around the soft edges
Of love and union.
Discovering who we are now,
Remembering who we were
When our hearts beat in a different lifetime,
Our souls danced to a different song,
But our love remained the same.
Over how many lifetimes have we drank in the stars together?
How many times have I watched the sun rise on your face?
The moon dance in your eyes?
The softness of firelight touch your skin in the darkness?
Our bodies entwined,

Lost to one another,

Time disappearing,

Nothing else existing,

Only us.

Two souls who have found each other once more,

In one breath,

In one moment of decision,

When the world stopped turning

And spirit was watching,

Smiling and patiently waiting,

For the day when

My soul would recognise you

Before my eyes did.

When my heart beat faster

In recognition,

Of a love and union

That has crossed timelines,

Survived a thousand lifetimes,

And will survive a thousand more.

For my soul will always remember you

Before my eyes do.

SOUL CONTRACTS

The concept of Soul Contracts is something that is intrinsically linked to the karma that we experience and Shadow Work that we talked about earlier in this book. It is something that has sat nestled somewhere in the deepest recesses of my subconscious for as long as I can remember. It's like when you are trying to place someone's face, it's familiar somehow and yet you can't remember how you know them or how/if you might have met them before. It feels like the answer, the memory is just out of reach.

I believe that we all have a remembering somewhere within our subconscious of the contracts we made with other souls before we chose to return to this lifetime. The 'remembering' of these contracts that we made takes form in the way that our energy speaks to us when we meet someone.

We have all experienced that feeling of instant connection with someone, like we have known them for years, or just simply 'click' with one another right from the beginning. We have also probably experienced the very opposite, when we have taken an instant dislike to someone, even if we can't really justify why. Their energy just feels off somehow and our instincts tell us to give them a wide berth.

I will dive into the dynamics of different Soul Contracts shortly but first, let me share with you what I believe a Soul Contract to be.

As I have mentioned previously, I believe from my own experiences with Past-Life Regression Therapy, as well as through memories and visions that have been shown to me during meditations, that we all reincarnate into a new life, over and over again. The purpose of this is to expand our soul through the unique experience of being human on this planet. The expansion comes from the experiences and the lessons that we learn in each life that we reincarnate into, each lesson adding to the beautiful cosmic imprint of our soul – the part of us that is eternal.

I believe that as souls we are drawn to return here time and time again because the experience is so unique. Science tells us that everything is energy vibrating at different frequencies, and everything that we sense around us on Earth is vibrating within the same parameters of the frequency that we are on, therefore we are able to experience it, feel it and connect our senses to it.

On Earth, our energy (our soul) incarnates into a physical form and it's the pleasure that comes through physical form that is so unique and magnetic, drawing us back to Earth time and time again.

I also believe that in the duality that we experience as human beings, we are encouraged and challenged to return and see if we can improve ourselves, experience something differently and evolve each time as a human and as a soul.

In my last book, *Natural Magic for the Modern Goddess*, I talk about what it means to be Divinely Human, a balance of our humanness and the Divine (the soul) within us.

This is the challenge, and I believe that in order to continually challenge, grow, learn, experience and evolve as souls, we work together with other souls, creating an agreement that we will return into each other's lives, in whatever capacity and for however long in order to re-learn a previous life lesson that we have struggled with, or to learn a new one. The experience can be perceived as a positive one or a real struggle, but the key point is that both souls agree to it.

This is the Soul Contract.

If you want to know who your Soul Contracts are in this lifetime, you can simply take a look at the relationships in your life, past and present. The ones that have left the biggest impact, the biggest lesson, will be the main Soul Contracts and key players in your Soul Team that will undoubtedly have been with you for many lifetimes and not necessarily in the same relationship dynamic that you have with them now. Your husband in this lifetime may have been a brother, a sister, a best friend, a parent in other lifetimes but you can guarantee that the one dynamic in your Soul Contract that will always remain the same is the lesson you have chosen to support each other with.

I have found through the re-learning and remembering of the concept of Soul Contracts, that I am able to take a more balanced approach to the different relationships that enter my life. I am able to gain a much higher perspective and ultimately, as a woman who is always consciously growing and strengthening her connection to her Inner Goddess, I can appreciate every single relationship and connection that I make, whether it has been a happy and positive one, or whether it has absolutely tested and pushed me to my limits, and at times to what has felt like my breaking point. For the latter, I always remind myself with so much gratitude that the pain I experience is another lesson I have been given to learn and ultimately, another gift that my soul has gleaned and added to its many facets.

When you view difficult relationships from this perspective, it really does help you to find the inner peace, acceptance and strength to move forward with gratitude in your heart. It will stop the pain from festering and eating away at you, blocking you from trusting again, opening your heart again and ultimately from inviting more of the same dynamic into your life again until you understand the lesson behind the pain.

When you can move through the pain and emerge from the other side with an awareness of the strength that it has given you and gratitude for the person who has taught you the hardest of lessons, you will know that you will never have to re-visit that pain again. This links back to what I was sharing with you on the concept of karma.

Once the knowledge and understanding of Soul Contracts has woven and threaded its way back into your awakened memory, you will then understand that relationships were always pre-destined to be what they are/were and for the time that you both participated within them. Some Soul Contracts last a lifetime, others for a handful of years and some just a few short months or weeks.

When we truly understand and see these Soul Contracts for what they are and what they have taught us, for however long they were in our life, we will find a deeper and more swift acceptance that the relationship is over and it is time to move forward again, if indeed it is destined to end.

It is important to note here at this point that I am not suggesting you skip over the pain and the emotion that comes with the ending of a Soul Contract. Remember the chapter, 'The Observer'? Allow yourself to feel it all in order to integrate the lesson into your core, but teach yourself to step back and observe from the perspective of the observer when you feel like you are drowning and struggling to make sense of it all.

This point leads me nicely onto the next chapter about 'Regret', but before we do, I have a few short questions for you to consider when considering the Soul Contracts in your own life.

SOUL QUESTIONS

Looking back at your life up to the present, who would you say have been the main players in your life's Soul Contracts so far? These key players will be those that have held the biggest influence, where you can see that this influence has shaped the course of your life's direction.

When you think of these main players in your Soul Contracts, are there any that you feel you have unresolved emotions and feelings towards? If so, why do you think this is?

Think about what you have learnt from these Soul Contracts that have left you feeling unresolved in some way. What gift did they bring to your life at the time and leave you with afterwards even if you didn't recognise it as such at the time? Consciously change the narrative from what they took from you, to what they gave to you, i.e., strength.

I believe that there are two types of Soul Contract:

1. Personal Soul Contract

2. Shared Soul Contract

Often, the two are entwined with one another. For example, I believe that while we are sat between lives, having returned to Source to re-group, evaluate our experiences from the life that we have just left, and consider what we want to learn and experience in the next life, we draw up a Soul Contract with our soul, a contract that commits us to achieving our true purpose and fulfilling karmic lessons. Once we have established the basic outline for how we want our life to be and what experiences we wish to be the main focal points, we draw in our Shared Soul Contractors to help us complete our mission. Each shared Soul Contract is mutually beneficial in supporting the growth of both souls.

Examples of shared Soul Contracts could be:

- Personal relationships, i.e., wife, husband or long-term partner

- Parental figures

- Siblings

- Teachers

- Friendships

This list is not limited to these examples. As I mentioned earlier, Soul Contracts usually tend to be the relationships or connections we have made that have had a significant influence on our perception of life at the time which has then created a shift in the direction of our life's path.

SOUL QUESTION

Imagine for a moment that you are considering your new personal Soul Contract before you enter your current lifetime. What do you think you wanted your main lesson and achievement to be in this lifetime? Journal on what thoughts come up for you around your answer.

BALANCE OF THE DIVINE MASCULINE & DIVINE FEMININE

To fully embody our Divine Feminine is to fully embody our Divine Masculine in equal measure.

I wrote this chapter on the eve of the Summer Solstice and the day after I celebrated with one of my fellow soul sisters at the annual Soul Escape Festival here in Lincolnshire.

This day also happened to be Father's Day here in the UK and so it was that I sat tucked up with my morning cuppa in bed as the dawn broke, contemplating my very own and deeply complicated relationship with the Divine Masculine in my life.

I woke this particular morning with tired and aching knees after a day of transformation, yoga and healing dance that had left me with the most profound sense of inner peace, joy and a lightness to my soul that I had not felt for a long time.

As my soul sister Ruth and I danced in the rain, moving our bodies in the most gloriously intuitive way, jumping, stamping our feet, swaying our hips, weaving our arms, allowing our bodies to flow in time with the beat of the music, I had felt the last vestiges of the shadows from my past fall away. I danced them out of me, and

I can't tell you how euphoric and free I felt.

As I sat that morning and contemplated the words that I wanted to share on this special day with my father, and also with the father of my children, I was drawn to consider the journey that I had been on, not only with the men in my life but with my own complex relationship to the Divine Masculine.

This life has seen me dive deep into re-connecting, re-claiming and honouring the Divine Feminine within me, my Inner Goddess. My last book, along with this one, is a dedication to the DF within us all, however, I am only just recently starting to forge a sacred and trusting relationship with the DM within and around me for the first time at 41 years old.

The last decade of my life has watched me unveil revelation after revelation regarding my dysfunctional relationship with the DM. In my last book, I shared with you my discovery that every major decision that I had ever made in my life up until my early thirties had been made to honour a man's happiness rather than my own. I also believed that in order to create a successful life I had to drive away the emotion and the feminine in my work, focussing instead on drive, climbing the ladder and choosing a traditional career in order to call myself a success in other people's eyes.

This is not to say that choosing a traditional career and wanting to climb the ladder is the wrong choice, not at all, but if your decisions come from a sense of obligation placed upon you by society rather than choosing the path that your heart truly wishes to follow, you are going to potentially lose that beautiful, intuitive connection to your Inner Goddess – your Divine Feminine.

As I dove deeper into self-preservation mode for the sake of healing my DF I began to view the men in my life in a negative light. I began to perceive any 'masculine' way of doing things – whether it was choosing a career, being deeply driven to succeed, or honouring a man's needs over my own – from a deeply negative and resentful perspective. There was no part of me that wished to share my life with a man any longer. There was no part of me that wished to please a man or work with men. I wanted only to find my soul's nourishment from surrounding myself with women who were committed to their own healing journey and honouring their own Inner Goddess.

Over time I witnessed myself becoming bitter towards men, resentful with no part of me prepared to honour and respect their opinions and listen to their message when an attempt was made to share it with me or others. I believed that I had wasted too much of my precious time and energy already on men and had my fingers burnt time and time again.

Well, not anymore!

The next chapter of my life was about honouring myself and only the Inner Goddess within me. I had officially moved from living my life with a major imbalance of the Divine Feminine to a major imbalance with the Divine Masculine, too fixated on my belief that my strength would come only from honouring Her.

As I sit and reflect upon all of this as I share with you, I feel my heart opening fully and truthfully to this predicament that I had come to find myself in, at a time in my life when I believed that my relationship with my IG was all that I needed in order to be happy and live a balanced and content life.

Time and again the message that I have been receiving from within myself is to open up my heart, let down my barriers and allow my heart to give and receive love as it was always meant to. I had ignored the deeper message that whispered below the surface, nor did I fully comprehend that because my heart was closed, I was shutting out the DM in all forms.

This epiphany came as I danced all the negative crap out of my body at the Soul Escape Festival surrounded by the unifying energy of love and joy that emanated within this space from the men and women that danced alongside me. Strangers drawn together at the same time to hold space only for joy, only for now, only for that moment in time. As the music danced its way into my body, heart and spirit, my soul began to expand until it felt as if it were bursting out of my body. As I allowed every possible emotion to rise within me, I let it go with every beat of the music.

I didn't just watch the souls around me do the same, I felt them do the same. It was like we were shedding and dancing off the last of the sludge that had kept us feeling heavy as we turned towards the sun and the celebration of the life that is so abundant within and around us with the season of Summer.

I made beautiful connections at the Soul Escape festival with both men and women, and it was exactly what I needed to spark the shift and the healing of my Divine Masculine.

The energies of the Divine Masculine and Feminine do not only apply to human men and human women. These two energies are the Yin and Yang of Universal energy that are needed to create life in all its forms. Both energies have their own unique set of energetic blueprints that can be linked mindfully to the way that we think, feel, act and do. We can get really specific and tap into one energy or the other when we are looking to harness success in certain endeavours. For example, in astrology, the sun is associated with masculine energy because masculine energy is active energy that likes to 'do', is confident and assertive. The moon is associated with the feminine and is associated with emotion, intuition, wisdom and heart-centred energy. Think about it like this: during the summer months, the sun is at its highest and strongest and life is abundant, busy and at its very peak performance in nature. At night when the moon makes her appearance, we tend to slow right down, ready to rest and settle into what feels good for us after a long and busy day. We eventually disappear into the dream world where our subconscious and intuition can often work at their peak while we sleep.

Let's take a look at a quick overview of the energies that both the DM and DF gift us with, and as we do, we can begin to notice how they both interweave with one another so that balance and harmony are found. When there is balance between both, there will ultimately be unity and equilibrium found in all creation.

DM Attributes	DF Attributes
Boundaries	Freedom
Confidence	Heart-centred
Risk-taking	Intuitive
Discipline	Gentle
I AM	WE ARE
Yang	Yin
Assertiveness	Compassionate
Action	Gentle
Logic and reason	Wisdon
Survival	Creative

TASK

Take a look now at the lists and circle the attributes that you have. Do you notice that you have more DF or DM attributes, or a beautiful balance of both?

Where might you find more balance between them?

Look at the ones that you haven't circled now. Consider how the absence of these attributes has possibly impacted your life. Journal on your thoughts.

LOVE - REFLECTIONS & SUMMARY

Throughout this Pillar, we have created solid foundations of love, commitment and boundaries that will support our Inner Goddess as she continues to rise. We understand the importance of never losing sight of how far we have come to bring our Inner Goddess to the top of the Pillar, but when it comes to the relationship with our self and with others, we also understand how important it is to seek balance by honouring both the Divine Masculine energies and the Divine Feminine energies. Our Universe and life itself can only thrive when the two work harmoniously with one another.

Working on the Love Pillar is a continuous journey where vigilance is key. Once we accept that we are always a work in progress when it comes to working with and maintaining our strong relationship with our Inner Goddess, we will understand how important it is to stay committed to ourselves and the five Pillars, not just for a chapter but for a lifetime.

SOUL QUESTIONS

Where have you placed your Goddess philosophy so that you can see it every day?

Are you finding it easy to stick to your boundaries since reviewing and renewing them in this Pillar?

Have you noticed any changes within the dynamic of your relationships since strengthening your boundaries?

Has your newfound understanding of Soul Contracts helped you to find peace and gratitude for someone who has played a difficult role in your life?

Do you feel that you have lived your life with more Divine Masculine or Divine Feminine, or a good balance of both? Explain your answer.

PILLAR FIVE

$\rightarrow\!)\!\bullet\!(\!\leftarrow$

FREEDOM

Congratulations, beautiful Goddess. You have reached the final Pillar, the Pillar of Freedom, and this is where your Inner Goddess is free to roam, wild and unfettered as the true Goddess that she is. The other four Pillars are very much focused on our inner world while Freedom focuses on aligning with our outer world. Shifting and realigning with our inner world means that we will want to shift and realign some aspects of our outer world, this way we can offer our Inner Goddess the beauty of the Universe that she so deserves.

Finding freedom within finds freedom with-out. Our oneness with nature, our planet and the seasons, the moon and the cosmos is a connection that we humans have been nurturing since the dawn of our time here on Earth. When we remember that we are not separate from but in fact a part of the world around us, we will feel our energy begin to shift and flow with the seasons and the cosmos more freely, bringing more balance to our health and wellbeing as well as keeping our Inner Goddess connected as the magical bridge that she is between heaven and Earth.

Within this Pillar, we will understand what it means to find freedom as a Goddess, and we will explore the parts of the land that call to our Inner Goddess. We will embody living in a way that is present rather than with regrets, and we will dive into the powerful magic of Astrology that has whispered starry messages and guidance to our ancestors since we first looked up at the sky.

Are you ready to embrace your freedom, Goddess?

FREEDOM TO BE A GODDESS

For your Inner Goddess to truly shine and guide you through life as your most authentic expression of who you are, you must allow her freedom – freedom to breathe, freedom to speak, freedom to express, freedom to feel, freedom to step away from what is deemed normal by society, freedom to choose, freedom to love, freedom to create, freedom to say no, freedom to explore the world and ultimately, freedom to fully explore and understand herself on every level and in every situation.

So many of us feel a lack of freedom in our lives as we become bound by the constraints of work and the career progression that we wish to achieve. We invest in a home for ourselves and our family, and the sense of exploration and adventure and 'let's give something new a go' slowly disappear over time as we reiterate to ourselves that we are getting older, we now have responsibilities and it's time to get serious about life. After all, we can't just please ourselves and do what we want without a solid life plan forever, can we?

There is a certain expectation when we move past our mid-twenties to start settling down into a career, a home of our own, start making plans for a family and basically, in a nutshell, screw the nut and get serious about life.

But who says that life has to be this way? Who says that we must do things in a certain order in life for it to make sense and be deemed an acceptable way of living and progressing as a human being?

I'm not saying that this isn't an acceptable way of progressing through life, by the way, not at all. My point that I'm getting around to is that:

1) It is ok to do life your way, in a way that feels right for you, and

2) It is important to check in regularly with yourself and where you are at in life in order to create awareness of whether or not the structures that you have created in your life still feel like they fit, they work and they feel good for you.

As natural creatures of habit, we can drift on autopilot for a while, struggling with feelings of restriction and frustration and lack of time but without considering changing anything simply because we have always lived our life this way.

But what if life just doesn't feel good anymore?

What if your goals and aspirations have changed?

What if you feel the urge or desire to try something different?

What if you find that you have fallen completely out of love with your life or your partner?

If we ever question why we feel restricted or stuck in our circumstances, we can so easily choose to paper over the cracks and tell ourselves that how we are feeling is 'normal' and that we have no real justification for feeling as miserable and as ungrateful as we do. But what justification is acceptable when it comes to choosing our own happiness? Why is it far easier and justifiable to walk away and quit on the heels of a major drama, betrayal or – God forbid – wakeup call that has us questioning our mortality? Why does life have to reach that level of intensity before we decide that we are justified in looking for a change that makes us happy?

To fully embrace the Goddess within and the Goddess that you truly are, to live the life that you deserve and to enjoy the happiness and contentment that you have every right to experience for the short time that you have been planted here on this Earth, your Inner Goddess must be allowed to embrace the freedom that she craves, that makes her smile, that lights her up, that sparks her creativity, that ignites her inner lover and that wants to do life her way and on her terms.

So often the lack of freedom that we feel does not come from an external influence, it comes from the constraints that we choose to accept and place upon ourselves.

We have a choice.

We can choose our freedom.

We can choose another way.

We can choose to do life differently.

We can free ourselves of misplaced guilt over not wanting what everyone else has got or the pressure of keeping up appearances for the sake of everybody else's expectations or opinions.

It is simple. We can choose happiness.

We can choose to be free.

We just have to say YES to our Inner Goddess.

SACRED PILGRIMAGE

*'Your soul whispers to the land and the land
whispers to your soul.'*

There is a weaving, an intertwining between all five of the Goddess Pillars, but for me, all five can often feel most palpable all at once when I visit the lands that call to my soul and my spirit.

I believe that there is at least one very special corner of this planet, however big or small, that calls to our Inner Goddess to visit in order to offer us healing and reconnection to ourselves and the world around us. Finding this sacred space and allowing our Inner Goddess to rest and rejuvenate within the energy of these places is imperative for the continued growth and nourishment of our Inner Goddess as she evolves through life and her experiences.

In 2021, four months after ending my marriage, I took my first pilgrimage to a place that has called to my heart for a very long time. I knew that when I finally got the chance to go, it would be on a solo adventure that was deeply personal to me and one that would be pivotal to my healing, uncovering my deepest truths, bursting my heart wide open with love that had been held for too long, and reconnecting me to my freedom that had been waiting patiently for me to grab it with both hands at long last!

After a painful and turbulent time of transition and untangling myself from my marriage, fighting against every fear-induced response to take back the decision I had made to separate my family because I couldn't face the guilt that I was so heavily burdened with for being the one to make the decision that would alter four lives forever, I packed a bag and got into my car. My destination was Glastonbury in Somerset.

I left Lincoln feeling completely broken, exhausted and lost, but as each mile flew beneath me taking me further and further away from my hometown, I felt the pressure in my lungs and my chest ease, little by little. I felt the heaviness begin to lift. I felt freedom calling for me at the top of her lungs.

I had spent a large portion of my life living on the south coast, mostly in Dorset and Hampshire, but had only ever passed through Somerset on my way to visit my brother in Exmouth or on family trips to Cornwall. I couldn't explain at the time why it was that I felt such a pull to this part of the country as I really didn't know much about it at all until one day when my dad told me that he had been tracing our family tree and had managed to follow it right back to Somerset where our Viking ancestors had settled centuries ago. I work a lot with ancestral energy and healing within my work with my clients and strongly believe that we hold energetic cords within our body that connect us to the wisdom, memories, trauma and lessons experienced by the generations who have come before us. I will talk more about this in a later chapter but for now, I could consciously honour the connection that I so clearly had through my Viking heritage to this part of the world, and I felt as if I was experiencing a returning of sorts as I made my journey south along the long and endless stretch of M5 motorway.

As I turned off the motorway heading deep into the Somerset countryside, I could feel the fizzing and popping of energy in every cell of my body as my destination drew closer with every moment. The rolling green hills and winding country roads carried me straight into the heart of Avalon and when my eyes first caught sight of Glastonbury Tor in the distance, my heart skipped a beat. It felt like a magical lighthouse guiding me to shore and safety.

As I turned onto the main high street of Glastonbury, I slowed right down to take in the colourful assortment of new-age shops with windows full to the brim with crystals of every kind, witchy books galore ready for diving into in little independent bookshops, and holistic health stores showcasing their magical herbal potions and remedies, incenses and oils. The sun had disappeared behind the clouds, but the world felt like it was bright and shiny suddenly and I couldn't wait to find my B&B, drop my bags and head back into town to explore before the last of the daylight hours faded away.

I had managed to find the perfect room in a wonderful place just off the high street and a ten-minute walk from the Tor, Chalice Well and the White Spring. I had decided to splash out a little and treat myself to the Queen Suite in the garden room that came with its own rolltop bath with a view through the vines of a willow tree just outside the window (my favourite tree). Beyond the willow was an established and elegant rose garden (my favourite flower, and another sign from the Universe that this was where I was meant to stay) which had seating around a fire pit at the back. It was utterly peaceful and such a beautiful sight that I really felt quite emotional as I took a deep breath in and took a moment to centre myself within the magic of it all.

Glastonbury is steeped in deep and magical myths and legends that can find their roots in the Dark Ages and the time of King Arthur, who is said to have been buried in Glastonbury.

This quirky little town in the middle of Somerset is a world-renowned place of pilgrimage because it is believed by many to sit at the heart of the Earth's energy lines that map the entire planet. The heart chakra energy that resides here is connected to the Divine Feminine energy that is believed to reside in all things, along with the Divine Masculine. This Divine Feminine energy is perhaps felt more prevalently in Glastonbury due to the connection that it holds with Mary Magdalene who is believed to have visited this most sacred place with Joseph of Arimathea and the Holy Grail after the resurrection of Christ. For worshipers of pagan faith and origins, it is said that Glastonbury was a place of pre-Christian worship, a place in which the Goddess and her Feminine wisdom and beauty were seen and felt so prevalently within the rolling hills and curves of Mother Earth. This little town is also believed to be the gateway to the mythical Isle of Avalon of ancient Celtic mythology and is believed to be the place that King Arthur's Excalibur was forged.

When I arrived in Glastonbury, I knew very little about the history and the legends surrounding the town and can only say that it was my heart and my intuition that had guided me here for healing.

My stay in Somerset was a true calling back home to myself on every single level. As I climbed the Tor to catch the first and last rays of the sun that blanketed the Earth below as far as the eye could see, I felt the whispers of my ancestors on the breeze that rustled through my hair. As I soaked my skin in the healing waters of the sacred White Spring, I felt cleansed of all hurt and pain, with a sense of renewed spirit and a re-birthing of sorts washing over me.

During my few days in Glastonbury, I sat and wrote chapters of this book in the Chalice Well Gardens, knowing that the ancient magic of the Goddess that resides so strongly here would infuse itself into the pages as I wrote. I visited the Goddess Temple in the centre of the town and spent hours in this incredible space dedicated solely to the worship of Goddess. Within its sacred walls I was cleansed and welcomed into the very heart of Goddess where I sat and meditated in between writing more of my book. I have never experienced such peace as I have in this place.

At 39 years old, this was the first time in my life that I had taken a vacation on my own. It was the most liberating experience and one that now had me hooked on solo adventures. I had longed for freedom and space for so long, a freedom that felt like I was reconnecting back to myself, a freedom that reminded me of who I was without being someone's wife and mother, but I had never allowed myself to take it.

As a notorious people pleaser, I so desperately just wanted some time to do as I pleased without always agreeing to someone else's demands just because it made life easier. This is why travelling on my own has become so addictive, I don't want to take anyone else into consideration because I have been doing it all my life. Now, I just want to honour and indulge my Inner Goddess who has gone without her freedom for too long.

The trip to Glastonbury was to be the first of many to come, and over the next two years of my life, I indulged in travel and adventure to some beautiful places, some with my girls and some solo that called to my soul to plant myself there and experience the incredible beauty of the planet that we are so lucky to call home. In doing so, I'd call myself back home to my Inner Goddess each and every time, with each new experience, new culture, new climate and unknown land gifting me a deeper and more aligned perspective on life and what I wanted from it, what I wanted to change and what would remain the same.

One of my very closest friends, Kimberley, is the most phenomenal healer and hypnotherapist, having trained in Quantum Healing Hypnosis Technique, which includes but is not limited to facilitating past life regression. While she was studying and training, I had the absolute honour and privilege of being a case study for Kimberley, and it was through the incredible journeys that took me back to many different past lives that I formed the belief that we are drawn to certain places because there is often a strong link to a past life. I believe that the land, the very Earth of places and spaces, holds its own unique energy which when woven with the rich history of all who have ever walked and lived and loved and fought and birthed in these places makes them simply magnetic.

These places hold an energy that calls to our soul, our spirit and our body on a level that we might not always be aware of or fully comprehend, however, this energy of that very particular piece of the planet is letting you know that you need it in order to reconnect, in order to heal, in order to learn and also to let go and evolve.

Your soul may feel called to visit many different places all over the world or it may feel called to re-visit the same place time and time again. This very magnetic piece of the Earth may even be a stone's throw from your doorstep. It might even be your home itself. Wherever it may be, it is a place that calls you back to yourself, back to your peace, back to clarity, back to nature perhaps and ultimately back to your Inner Goddess. It acts like a reset button every single time and you realise that you need it in your life as often as possible.

SOUL QUESTIONS

Is there a special place that calls you to visit often?

Do you allow yourself the freedom to visit as much as possible? Explain your answer.

How does that special place make you feel when you are there or when you think about going?

Is there somewhere that has always pulled at you to visit and explore? Take some time to research this place and perhaps commit to planning a visit.

S-H-E

Are you S – H – E, the Sacred Healer of Earth?

Do you feel the call of our Great Mother?

Do you feel connected, protective and empowered by the land?

Do you hear her whispers?

Her song?

Her wisdom, ancient and wise, flowing through your veins?

Are you her sacred keeper, entrusted with the wise ways?

Your ancestors' blood reminding you of who you once were, are and will always be.

Earth Witch,

Medicine Woman,

Maiden, Mother and Crone.

Entrusted with your sacred position,

Healer of Earth,

Keeper of old ways,

Plant whisperer,

Tree lover,

Sorceress,

Protectress of Gaia.

Your soul will always feel the call,

Your spirit will always hear the whispers,

Your body will always feel the pulse.

For you are S – H – E

And S – H – E is Gaia.

No time for regret

This chapter is far more of the 'short and sweet' variety compared to the chapters on Shadow Work and Soul Contracts. This is because the concept of having no regrets really is quite a simple one to reach after processing the work in the aforementioned chapters.

When we understand fully that everything that we have experienced in life has ultimately been for our highest good, our ultimate growth and evolution, and that we agreed to experience these situations within our Soul Contracts and subsequent karmic lessons, then how can we possibly regret anything that we experience? How can we possibly think that things could have, should have been different?

Everything that we experience, everything that has come to be, once was, and is ever unfolding in front of us is exactly how it is meant to be, simply, because it has happened. If it wasn't meant to be then it wouldn't have happened.

It really is that simple.

A clue to the karmic lessons that will follow us potentially into the next lifetime will be the ones hidden behind the concept of 'regret' that we take with us when our soul departs from its earthly realm.

Viewing every situation in life as another lesson, another gift, another opportunity to understand ourselves and what we want and need on an even deeper level than ever before will always leave us feeling fulfilled and, more importantly, help to keep us present and grounded in reality and how we choose for our reality to unfold.

If you know and trust that despite everything that has gone before, in this moment you are exactly where you are meant to be, having experienced everything that you were meant to experience, then you will uncover the very deepest sense of contentment and appreciation for this crazy thing we call 'Life'.

You will experience the ultimate sense of freedom that will come from diving fully into every experience knowing that it was always meant to happen this way, and you will feel the deepest connection to Spirit, your Inner Goddess, the Cosmos and your purpose.

SOUL QUESTION

Imagine that this is your last day on Earth and you are looking back on your life. Do you think that you would look back and experience the feeling of regret for what you should have/would have/could have done differently?

This is your unresolved karma. Take this opportunity to make peace with how your life has turned out, dig deep and find the gratitude for the gift and the lesson. If you feel that something needs addressing or changing in your life, it's never too late – pledge an oath to your Inner Goddess right now to take action.

EMPOWERING YOUR INNER GODDESS WITH ASTROLOGY

The mantra that I try to remember when I commit to anything in life is that it will only be successful if there is balance. For something to flourish and find its equilibrium, there must always be a delicate balance of energies that are not always easy to achieve but are there to be captured and honoured nonetheless.

As you will know by now, my journey down my own spiritual path of self-discovery began with reconnecting my energy in a conscious way back to Mother Earth and her seasons. From there, I also began to weave the cycles and the phases of the moon into my daily rituals and practices, but it would take me over a decade before I would find myself embarking upon a journey that I never saw coming in my wildest dreams.

As my work with Natural Me began to unfold and evolve, so too did my interest in our heavens. I guess now that I'm sharing this part of my journey with you it seems obvious that my path would naturally lead me deeper into astrology, but somehow, I never saw this part of my journey in my overall vision for my online community.

One of my most favourite offerings within the Natural Me Community is my monthly edition of Cosmic Nature – a monthly guide and journal to the season, stars and planetary influences which, as I think back to try and remember where this gorgeous offering began to form in my mind's eye, I can't seem to remember at all. It just simply appeared one day having flowed right out of me from the personal learning and knowledge that I had undertaken along the path of my own evolution.

As I began to sink my teeth into more and more of Cosmic Nature's magic, I wanted to build on my very basic astrology knowledge and so it was that I found the Silver Spiral Goddess Astrology Course facilitated by my starry Goddess and cosmic wisdom keeper, Maria Jones that kicked off its two-year Star Priestess training on none other than the day of my 40th solar return. If this wasn't a big, fat, starry sign from the Universe then I would eat my own hat.

Becoming an astrologer has felt like finding the Yin to my Yang. Having spent a decade creating a very conscious way of living with Earth and her seasons, I have now created an equally epic and important relationship with our stars and planets. I am connected above and below and life feels good, it feels balanced and what is more, I feel like I have called home to me the last humungous piece of ancient wisdom that I have nurtured many times over since my soul found its place on this Earth.

For most of us, our astrology knowledge extends as far as knowing our star sign, which is in fact our Sun Sign, and understanding the general energetic overview of the qualities that it lends us in our daily life. But oh my word... If only we all knew how little of the surface we scratch when it comes to our personal astrology.

Understanding our personal birth chart – a chart that gives us the exact placements of the planets and constellations the moment we were born – lends us a knowledge and perspective on ourselves and our nature that is so deep and so ancient that it is impossible to deny how accurate these starry maps are that represent our cosmic blueprint as timeless souls.   A   s an astrologer, I find myself diving down a rabbit hole of magic when I look at someone's chart and how it can offer my clients guidance and perspective on their life.

To share with you the magic of creating an entire birth chart would require a whole new book to be written, so, for the purposes of this beautiful journey into returning to your Inner Goddess, I wanted to share with you one seemingly small but in actual fact very intrinsic part of your personal astrology story and how you can learn to weave and honour it into the very essence of your Inner Goddess.

YOUR MOON SIGN

When we look into our own personal astrological blueprint, we start by looking at the Sun Sign – the overarching layer that gives us a sense of who a person is, their identity and personality traits. Our Sun Sign gives us an idea of our strengths and perceived weaknesses and our purpose that we came to fulfil in this lifetime.

If our Sun Sign is all about how we project ourselves outwardly, then our Moon Sign is about the layers of ourselves that are held within us, within our emotional and spiritual self. Our Moon Sign shines her soft light on what our soul craves most on an energetic level and is the place where our deepest woundings and traumas can be held amongst the shadows of our conscious and subconscious thoughts.

Our Moon Sign also represents our inner child and the nurturing that we did or did not receive in childhood. This is the place that resides within us that holds all of our childhood insecurities and energetic imprints that come from our parents and theirs before them.

We can see from our Moon Sign where we hold these shadows in our life and where the karmic patterns have spanned through generations as well as past lives. Understanding our own ancient lunar imprint and its place within our chart helps us to understand ourselves at the deepest level. Honouring our moon placement will honour our Inner Goddess, will heal her, will love her, will understand and empathise and will ultimately end cyclical emotional traumas and patterns so that we will never have to re-live them in another lifetime.

So, in order to find out what your moon placement is, you will need the following information, and it is very important that this information is precise:

- Your full name at birth
- Place of birth
- Exact time of birth

Once you have your information, you will need to access the internet and find a free birth chart website that will create your birth chart for you. I highly recommend Astroseek.com – super easy, it will literally do it all for you and guide you through putting in your info. It will then calculate your chart which will come up looking like a wheel or a circle with lots of different symbols on it. You will find your Moon Sign as a little crescent moon symbol on your chart. To understand its placement, scroll down to underneath the wheel and it will list the sign that each planet sits in. Once you know your Moon Sign you can find my interpretation of it here.

ARIES MOON - FIRE ELEMENT

Our beautiful moon is governed by the element of Water. Water is the element of the Divine Feminine whose energies are intrinsically linked to our emotions, our psyche and our intuition. Knowing this will forewarn you of what is held in store for you if you have a moon ruled over by Fire – the element representing the Divine Masculine and does exactly what it says on the tin – it fires things up!

As an Aries moon, you are a well-balanced and nurturing soul who thrives on walking your own independent path – the fact that it might not have been a path trodden before makes it all the more appealing to you. As a consequence, you inadvertently shine a light of inspiration to all those around you and enjoy supporting others with creating their own independence.

You are fiercely strong-minded and don't take kindly to those who make you feel like they are trying to rob you of your independence. Your creativity knows no bounds and you find that within these creative moments is where you find your true magic and purpose.

In relationships, you may struggle to maintain boundaries. This is a karmic lesson for you in this lifetime and you may tend to find that when your boundaries are constantly pushed against, you eventually explode – but more with anger and frustration at yourself for having let it continue for too long. This is usually the biggest reason that you can become quite aloof with people, preferring to keep others at arm's length.

The relationships that light you up are ones with those who have a similar outlook on life, who tend to take the bull by the horns and go for what they want. You can find yourself easily frustrated and lacking in understanding towards others who struggle to be what you would call 'proactive' with their goals. You are known to have a short temper when others' life admin encroaches on your time and you really don't like the feeling of being overwhelmed as this creates fear from a perceived lack of control.

Shadows from your childhood may run deep and reoccur throughout your life regarding your mother and her influence over you, particularly in childhood if you do not address the issues and return to an understanding that a lot of what you experienced and interpret are in fact a projection of her shadows onto you and indeed are not your responsibility at all.

TAURUS MOON - EARTH ELEMENT

To understand a Taurus moon and the aspects of life that their sense of stability and contentment come from, you need look no further than to observe their surroundings that they have built for themselves.

Signs and planets ruled over by the element of Earth are grounded in perspective and outlook on life, are practical thinkers and find comfort and pleasure from the finer things that life has to offer.

As a Taurus moon, you are deeply sensual and understand exactly what you need in terms of physical pleasure within your relationships. You are a Goddess between the sheets, however, you also have an extremely open heart and love to share emotionally intimate connections with others. Often this beautiful and loving facet of who you are can leave you feeling vulnerable when another does not return the same openness and heartfelt love in the way that you do. You may have a tendency to rush into love which can often lead to you getting burnt.

You feel most nurtured and safe when your finances are stable and when your daily routine is established and familiar. You take pride in having a beautiful home and enjoy spending time in it with those you love. Surrounding yourself with the finer things in life lights you up and makes you feel good but be careful not to put too much emphasis on nurturing your happiness from material possessions alone.

Gemini Moon - Air Element

As an Air sign, Gemini moons feel most at one with life when they are part of a community and network of people who hold space for them as equally as they themselves hold space for others.

Nurturing your mind and your intellect is where you find your happy place, and when you share this knowledge with others you feel like you are achieving collective growth and ultimately that you are being truly seen and heard, your sense of validation strengthened as your intellectual successes are recognised.

Your gift for being able to wear and try on many different proverbial hats is second to none but you can find it challenging to stay committed to seeing a project through to the end as this creates a flightiness to your attention span as you are always drawn to discovering and learning many new things. Structure and consistency are areas of life that you may need to work on to avoid scattiness and dropping the ball. This is particularly poignant when it comes to your commitment to loved ones.

Your personal relationships can often take a back seat due to your energy always seemingly scattered to the four corners, and more often than not, those around you struggle to know if you are coming or going. This does however add to your charm and your quirkiness but be mindful that you don't overstretch your time, energy and resources by taking on too much.

Cancer Moon - Water Element

This watery, feminine moon is in the sign of our Mother and Nurturer as she is recognised within the sign of Cancer. Cancer will find us right at the centre of our heart, she will honour us and love us unconditionally and she will help us to feel safe and secure.

As a Cancer moon, you will recognise that you have an absolute gift for reading a room. You are empathic and you have a heart that reaches out to everyone that you meet. You are renowned for your intuition never letting you down and this comes from your strong, psychic abilities, whether you acknowledge them or not.

Your favourite place to be is at home where you can just be yourself, rest, relax and potter about tending to your sacred home space and making it feel homely and safe.

You can often feel quite tired, battling with your energy levels having taken on a lot of other people's emotions while trying your best to support them, and this is something that you have to be mindful of. Remember to take time for yourself, don't over-give from an empty cup.

It is inevitable with a Cancer moon that you may often feel overwhelming emotions, taking many things to heart when feeling overly sensitive. Family means everything to you and you strive to nurture your relationship with those that you call family. If you grew up without the nurturing and loving influence of a mother then it is likely that you will have made it your mission to break this cyclical pattern within your lineage in order to be the best mother/wife/partner/friend/sister that you can be.

LEO MOON - FIRE ELEMENT

Another beautiful mix of creative and playful masculine energies with the loving and emotionally connected feminine energies. Leo is our little firecracker within the zodiac, here to roar loudly and proudly, to be seen AND heard!

As a Leo moon, you have confidence and charisma, you have energy and you are magnetic to your purpose and to others. You have a bold personality and enjoy the busyness that life has to offer, often found right at the centre of whatever is going on.

So often to the observer you are envied for the way you ease yourself into any situation with confidence and great conversation. However, others do not realise that, despite your colourful shell, there lies within a much softer and self-conscious side to you that you can keep hidden from the world for the most part until pushed too far and the inevitable fiery outburst is witnessed in all of its glory and magnitude.

Your Leo moon is here to always bring back the calm and perspective to your often hectic lifestyle. She is here to remind you of your insecurities and to witness and honour them, don't push them down because they make you feel less-than. Allow your inner child to run free and seek out joy, but don't throw a tantrum when you don't get your own way. Consider what makes you feel insecure when you react this way.

Virgo Moon - Earth Element

Virgo is our solace, our port in a storm when the world outside is crazy. As a Virgo moon, you seem to be everybody's comfort, everybody's deep, relaxing breath out when life becomes all too much. You have an incredible gift for helping others to feel whole again with your natural abilities and interests in the healing and holistic arts. Although you are insular by nature and sink deeply into your own inner world, you like to keep life simple and fill your time with the things that interest you and that you are passionate about.

As a Virgo moon, you are excellent at maintaining presence which keeps you incredibly grounded, and you have the ability to handle busy and stressful situations with dignity and poise. However, your diligence can often leave you worn out if you don't take a break from going at something like a steam train.

Although you are an excellent organiser under pressure as well as someone who can pay attention to the finer details, you prefer your life to be filled with calm and order. Your wants and needs are simple, nourishing and wholesome, but if you can't achieve this in your life, or feel like your circumstances are getting in the way of you achieving your peace and order, you begin to feel like you are losing control and this makes you feel anxious and irritable. Your true happy place is when you are pottering in your favourite space, listening to the sound of silence with hours of your own time stretched out ahead of you.

Libra Moon - Air Element

Oh Libra, the sign of love, equality, balance and relationships, how you set the stage for bliss that can only be found within the union of love, and the pain and destruction that this same love can bring.

As a Libra moon, you are here to learn, love and grow your soul through your relationships with others in this lifetime. You are here to show others what it means to embody diplomacy and fairness, as well as what it means to honour your boundaries and find balance between loving and being loved. It is so easy to love you, and yet so often you fall short of loving yourself the way that you truly deserve. Your biggest lessons in this lifetime will come from honouring yourself and laying karmic patterns to rest once and for all. These lessons will more than likely come in the form of creating stronger boundaries as you tend to be a natural 'giver', which is beautiful but can so easily be taken advantage of if you don't set the stage early in your relationships to show that you value your own wants and needs too.

Your relationships mean everything to you, making your world go round, and you will always try your hardest to keep the peace, but be careful that you don't compromise on your own happiness in order to do so. Trust that those who are deserving of loving you and receiving your love will continue to love you when you need to take a stand and be heard. Don't be afraid to use your voice!

Scorpio Moon - Water Element

Scorpio can so often get a bad rap for how intense things seem to get when they are around, and yet, this sign is here to offer us some of the deepest reflective healing and lessons in life that ultimately bring us the biggest rewards.

As a Scorpio moon, your waters run deep. You are the deepest of thinkers and can experience your emotions in an intense and overwhelming way when you allow them to run away with you. You have a tendency to internalise, but those who know you witness how much you care and love the ones that you hold closest to you.

There is a fiercely protective and loyal side to you but be careful that this doesn't become too overbearing and controlling for others to handle. Your insecurities can also run deep like scars that never quite heal beneath the surface, and you may have a tendency to struggle to admit when you are wrong. You would rather lash out than admit that you feel vulnerable.

There is an inner strength to you that knows no bounds and you pride yourself on your self-sufficient nature. You keep your inner circle small and your personal life is exactly that: personal. Something to keep in mind is that for love and relationships to thrive there must be an equal exchange of energies on both parts, so if you tend to keep your cards close to your chest, don't expect someone else to be an open book with you.

SAGITTARIUS MOON - FIRE ELEMENT

Sagittarius is the truth-seeker, the deep thinker, the freedom-finder and the philosophical teacher of life. There is so much about this sign that holds the energies of all of the elements so strongly within its grasp that I often wonder whether the ancient mystics and stargazers got it wrong when they decided to associate Fire as the element for this sign. The fact that I verbalised this thought will no doubt be seen as blasphemous, however, for me the element of Air stands out so strongly that it's always the first element that I'm drawn to connecting with for Sagittarius.

With a Sagittarius moon, your spirit soars high when you are free to follow your heart and what lights you up. You were never meant to follow a predictable path in life and therefore can often be found wandering through the landscapes that call most deeply to your soul's nourishment.

You are a deep thinker and your gift is for being able to reach your mind and your senses below the surface of any situation to discover the truth of what really lies within. You also have your sights set above you, aimed at the infinite sky and Universe, allowing yourself to be guided by something greater, something more expansive than just what we see and what we know here on Earth. You feel most nourished when you are learning and studying and developing a deeper understanding to the meaning of life.

Your experiences are your teachings and you light up at being able to share your experiences and your wisdom with others.

Spontaneity and travel to new places, new lands and cultures helps you to expand your consciousness and sink deeper into the lessons that you have come here to learn. Your community and network are testament to how much you are loved and respected for living and embodying your deepest truths.

Some of your biggest lessons in life might come from understanding that there must be a balance between committing to your inner, personal journey and staying present and enjoying the little moments in life, especially with those you love.

Capricorn Moon - Earth Element

Capricorn is the wise grandfather energy of the zodiac, stoic and dependable, grounded and safe, wise from experience and supportive and practical in times of uncertainty.

Your moon in Capricorn offers you the gift of being able to support yourself independently through the ability to create strong structures and systems in your life that stand the test of time. Your structures and boundaries keep you feeling nurtured and safe and you are known for giving the best and most practical advice when it is needed and perhaps emotions are running too high that either yourself or others can't see the wood for the trees.

You are an island that survives and thrives within your own ecosystem, and this in itself commands natural respect from those around you. You often come across as a little aloof, cold and quite clinical in your approach to life but this is how you function and are able to keep things in life manageable and streamlined. You thrive on order and consistency, however, be mindful that life is for living too. Enjoy the freedom that comes from being a self-sustaining island. Let your hair down and embrace more of your emotional side. Pushing away your feelings will only leave them to fester, creating problems and emotional blocks further down the line. Capricorn is a king when it comes to unravelling karmic lessons. Be sure to leave no stone unturned in this lifetime as you will only have to come back and attempt to face them once more in the next one.

Aquarius Moon - Air Element

As an Aquarius moon, you came here to break the mould, you came here to be the fullest expression of your most authentic self and you make no apologies about it.

Aquarius holds the codes of the stars and the Universe within her, meaning that she comes to Earth as a visionary and guide for herself and for others who wish to join her.

Your Aquarius moon means that you have no doubt felt like the round peg in the square hole at some point in your life, never feeling like you quite fit in anywhere which can often leave you forever searching for your place in the world.

You can often come from a place of detachment to situations which in fact lends you a deeper and more wise and balanced perspective and approach to situations, particularly difficult ones.

You are a loner and you are a conscious part of the collective. You are individual and yet you see yourself as the same. You understand that you are no better or no less than another. You are you and understand the importance of bringing your individuality to every encounter, every situation, in order to shine a light for others to do the same, ultimately raising the vibration of consciousness on the planet.

You feel most nurtured when you strike a balance between solo adventure as well as feeling the loving embrace of community with like-minded others. You feel most content within the space of personal freedom to choose your own path, but don't forget that life is for sharing with others along the way too!

Pisces Moon - Water Element

Pisces holds the wisdom of all twelve signs because she is the last sign to enter our zodiac wheel. She is the bridge between humanity and divinity and her soul runs deeply throughout everything she focuses her energy towards.

As a Pisces moon, you will feel life deeply, you will experience life deeply and you will love everyone with a heart that feels the needs of the whole collective.

Your empathy knows no bounds which makes others feel safe to be themselves and share their vulnerabilities with you because you accept everyone for who they are.

You are the dreamer and the mystic, and you crave the watery realms of self-discovery and the space to tap into your inner calm and peace. Due to your empathic nature, being around others can easily drain you if you don't protect your energy and balance your time and how much you support others. You can either feel the need to save the whole world or you fall prey to being the victim who needs saving.

You feel most nurtured when surrounded by others who are sharing in something creative and fun with you. The vibe can carry you off into another time and space where your spirit soars. Your equilibrium is easily out of balance, however, if you don't maintain that balance with self-care and solitude and time doing the fun things with others that your soul needs in equal measure.

You are the rays of sunshine that cover the soft sunset skies at dusk and you are everyone's happy place.

YOUR ASTROLOGICAL
ELEMENT IS YOUR GIFT

Understanding the elements in our birth chart and which ones are dominant and which ones are lacking not only helps us to understand our biggest strengths but also our weaknesses. By acknowledging the spaces within the cosmic elements of our chart, we gain more clarity on why we might struggle in certain areas of our life and our health. This knowledge of our elemental make-up will help us to create more balance and harmony and flow in every aspect of our life.

You have already created your birth chart, so now let's take a look at where we can find the elements. If you look just below your birth chart wheel, to the right you will see a small box with the letters, F, A, E, and W down the left-hand side of four rows. There are three columns with the letter headings, C, F, and M, but we won't be focusing on the meaning of these as we are going to keep it as simple as possible. The letters down the left side represent the elements, Fire, Air, Earth and Water with each element governing a planet and Sun Sign within the astrological chart. Each element offers its own unique energetic signature and influence to its chosen planet and sign. So, by looking at how many placements we have of each element, we can see whether we have a dominant element, a bit of an equal balance between all of them, or a less dominant element. Perhaps there is an element that doesn't show up at all in your chart.

If we were to dive even deeper than we are about to into looking at each individual elemental placement and which sign and planet it was linked to, we would begin to really dive into specific areas of our life that relate to each placement and uncover even more of our cosmic story that shows us who we really are. For now though, let's take a look at the energies that each element represents and see if you resonate with them. Each symbol in each row represents one placement so this is where it will be useful to count up how many symbols in each element you have. This will then tell you which element is more/less/equally dominant for you in your chart.

What I tend to find when I am reading my clients charts who have a huge majority of one element is that they not only harness the strengths of this element but often struggle with the shadow aspects too, meaning for example that if they had a large majority of fire energy, they would be a naturally confident person but at times may have a tendency to exude too much confidence which makes them arrogant or perhaps seen by others as egotistical. As we look at each element I will share with you both the gift (strength) and the shadow (struggle) that is associated with it. Does your cosmic elemental makeup resonate with you? It is also important to mention that we are all human and to live within both the light and the shadow is what it means to live a human life. We are here to learn and grow from both our strengths and our shadows. There is nothing to be ashamed of if you feel that your shadow aspect comes through more than you would like with an element. Acknowledging the less desirable parts of ourselves is a courageous and brave thing to do. We are always a work in progress.

EARTH

The symbols associated with the element of Earth in your chart are the colour green. Earth energy is grounded, practical, focused, organised, artistic and driven to achieve. The shadow side to not having enough Earth energy is a lack of focus and motivation to get up and go, sluggish energy, stuck in your head – worrier, anxious, depressed.

Too much Earth energy can lead to burnout from overworking with not enough time for fun and adventure, overly ambitious, and unable to achieve unrealistic goals.

Earth signs – Taurus, Virgo, Capricorn

BALANCING YOUR EARTH ELEMENT

- Stand outside with your feet on the bare Earth to soak up the energy of Gaia and pull your energy out of your head.
- Create to-do lists to help you stay focused and reduce overwhelm.
- Walk in nature regularly and breathe in fresh air.
- Create daily mindful rituals.
- Take regular breaks throughout your day, away from work.
- Try not to control and micro-manage every little thing. Go with the flooooow.

AIR

Air is represented by the colour yellow in our chart and offers us the gifts of communication, freedom, liberation, adventure, problem-solving, intellect, and multi-tasking.

If there is a lack of Air element you may be prone to brain fog and struggles with decision making, being reclusive, poor communication, feeling trapped by your circumstances, wanting to run away rather than face your problems, trouble retaining new information and difficulty multi-tasking.

Too much of the Air element might find you constantly stressed having taken on too much, unable to focus on one thing at a time, anxious, easily over-stimulated, worrying a lot, giving too much and not receiving enough support for yourself.

Air signs – Gemini, Libra, Aquarius

BALANCING YOUR AIR ELEMENT

- Setting firm boundaries and learning not to say yes to everything, otherwise you will burn out.
- Stimulate your mind by learning something new.
- Make regular time for friends and socialising.
- Find a balance between adventure and home life.
- Enjoy time to yourself as well as with others.

FIRE

This element is represented by the colour red as shown in your little square elemental chart. Fire represents energy, drive, confidence, passion, joy, transformation, ambition and assertiveness. When you are in flow and connected to your fire element in a balanced way, you find it easy to embody the fire Goddess' gifts.

If you have very little fire, you may struggle with confidence and finding the natural resources within you to create drive, desire and change in your life. You may feel like you are lacking passion in certain areas or perhaps all areas of your life and have spent many a time wishing that you could summon up the courage to go for what you want.

If you have too much fire energy, you may have a natural tendency to be too pushy when it comes to getting what you want, perhaps not always taking into consideration other people around you. When you are feeling super confident and in your zone you may come across as a little too over-confident and perhaps even arrogant. You may have a tendency to be a bit of a bull in a china shop. Hot-headed might be another term that resonates as you may struggle with a short temper and lack of patience with others and general situations if things aren't going your way.

Fire signs – Aries, Leo, Sagittarius

Balancing Your Fire Element

- Take regular exercise to burn off excess energy.

- Enjoy moving your body – dance more!

- Tap into your natural creative abilities and create something new – paint, draw, write! Get inspired!

- Be mindful of being more patient with yourself and others.

- Step up as leader more often. You are a natural.

WATER

Water is represented by the colour blue in our chart and is known as the element of femininity. Her gifts are intuition, emotional intelligence, beauty, psychic ability, sensitivity, and she is heart-centred, hard-working and empathic.

Too little of the water element might have you struggling with lack of trust in your intuition, not enough drive to commit to what you want, a lack of focus or direction, and not enough of what you truly love in life.

Too much water might mean that you struggle with having an addictive personality to things like alcohol. You might struggle with being too open to others' emotions, taking them on as your own, as well as being susceptible to delusional thoughts, psychic attacks, and emotional over-sensitivity. You can tend to be emotionally over-bearing, and you may find it hard to strike a balance between following your heart and making choices that are sensible and rational. You can also be prone to depression and anxiety.

Water signs – Cancer, Scorpio, Pisces

Balancing Your Water Element

- Practising more intuitive exercise forms such as yoga and Qi Gong.
- Regular journaling to help you process emotions.
- Practice your intuitive skills and learn to read oracle or tarot cards.
- Find a balance between following your head and your heart.

- Eat lots of fresh fruit, veg, nuts and seeds for feminine health.

SOUL QUESTIONS

What is your most abundant element?

What element is least abundant?

Do you have a balance of elements?

How can you relate the information that you have learnt so far about elements to yourself?

ELEMENTS & HEALTH

Now that you have identified your dominant and less dominant elements within your chart and how they might relate to your sense of wellbeing, we are going to take a look at how an imbalance of each element might manifest itself physically within the body as a chronic condition.

The idea that the elements are connected to the energies of the body and its organs is a concept that has been around for thousands of years and is found within many ancient Chinese medicine traditions. Acupuncture, ayurveda and naturopathy are some holistic therapies that focus closely on the relationship that the body has to the elements. I have found that by identifying the element that is lacking with my clients, I can link it to problematic areas associated with that element and create a bespoke treatment for clients that combines reflexology, aromatherapy and womb massage.

Earth Element - Physiological Links

Bones – nails – teeth – skin – hair – tissues – muscles – stomach - spleen

If there is an imbalance of Earth element, it will show as a general weakness in the body, low calcium levels in the bones, weight loss and weight gain, obesity and muscular diseases, joint pain and issues with hips, knees, ankles and feet.

Air Element - Physiological Links

Movement – contraction and expansion – suppression and vibration – mood disorders

An imbalance of Air element can manifest as depression, anxiety, blood pressure problems, dry skin, problematic lungs, insomnia, lethargy, muscle spasms, bloating, trapped wind and constipation.

Fire Element - Physiological Links

Thirst – hunger – sleep – eyes – skin complexion – heart

An imbalance of Fire element can manifest as a fever, inflammation, too much heat or too cold within the body, excessive sweating, diabetes, slow absorption of nutrients, poor digestion, liver problems, heart and cardiovascular problems.

Water Element - Physiological Links

Kidneys – saliva – blood – sweat – urine – semen – reproductive/ fertility

An imbalance of Water can result in oedema, swelling of glands, excess mucus, sinusitis, blood thinning or clotting. The Water element is linked closely to the reproductive system and disorders in sexual health, also including sex drive.

BALANCING THE ELEMENTS PHYSIOLOGICALLY

Some of the best ways to support your body with restoring its natural balance are with holistic therapies such as reflexology, acupuncture, aromatherapy, massage, medical herbalism, naturopathy, homoeopathy, Chinese medicine and Ayurveda. I always recommend that you check that the practitioner is with a governing body, as this identifies them as having received the correct training and qualifications. You should find the logo and info on the practitioner's website.

Diet of course is a very important part of keeping our bodies healthy and full of vitality. Eating a balanced diet consisting of fruit, veg, meat, fish, seeds and nuts is essential. Cutting out or reducing processed foods, caffeine and refined sugar will help to keep our body, mind and spirit healthy and happy.

There are many different self-help tools and techniques out there that support health and wellbeing such as meditation, journaling, yoga and pilates. Fresh air and being outside is excellent for balancing and grounding into Earth energy and reducing stress and anxiety. Listening to your favourite music, dancing and moving your body with exercise boosts endorphins and not only improves your physical health but boosts your wellbeing. Movement is an excellent way of connecting to all of the elements!

Creating a routine of self-care is really important because it establishes time-out from the daily grind, even if it is just a few moments each day when you can hit the brakes on your nervous system running away with itself from everything on your to-do list.

ESSENTIAL OILS FOR ELEMENTAL BALANCE

I love to use essential oils to help support me with my elemental health. You can pop a few drops in a diffuser or your bath or you can create a rollerball with a carrier oil that you can add your essential oils to.

It is important to note that advice from an aromatherapist must be sought if you are pregnant or have a health condition that requires medication before using essential oils.

You can add 6-8 drops of essential oil to a burner or diffuser, 5-20 drops in a tablespoon of carrier oil such as coconut to your bath, up to 5 drops in a 10ml rollerball bottle of carrier oil such as sunflower or sweet almond.

Here are some of my favourites:

Earth – cypress, patchouli, pine, sandalwood

Air – frankincense, clary sage, rosemary, basil

Fire – black pepper, cinnamon, orange, cedarwood

Water – bergamot, geranium, lavender, rose

CRYSTALS FOR ELEMENTAL BALANCE

Crystals are another great way of working with the natural healing Earth energy that each crystal holds within them from the Earth where they were formed. There are many ways of working with crystals, but the simplest way is to keep your chosen crystal somewhere on your person and preferably close to your skin.

Before working with crystals there are a few things you must do first. Once you have bought your crystal you must cleanse it, charge it and set it with intention.

Energy from every person who has ever come into contact with your crystal, from the person who mined it to the person who sold it to you, will have left their energetic print on it, so it is important that you cleanse your crystal of all residual energies before you use it.

CLEANSING YOUR CRYSTAL

You can simply hold your crystal for a minute or two under running water or even better, let a natural spring wash over it. As you do this, imagine all the stale and gloopy energies attached to it washing away. This works well for tumbled (smooth) crystals but not for rough crystals as they are much more delicate. You can place your rough crystals on the Earth, imagining that all sludgy, gloopy energy is being drawn out of it and back into the Earth where it is neutralised. It is also important to note that not all crystals should get wet. Other alternatives to water cleansing could be to use incense and pass your crystal through the smoke for cleansing. Research your crystal first to identify the do's and don't's to cleansing.

Charging Your Crystal

Brown and earthy-coloured crystals love to be charged outside under natural sunlight, even if it's a cloudy day – just place them on the Earth and let the sun and nature do the rest. Charging a crystal is like charging up its battery and energising it. When a crystal is taken away for long periods of time from the Earth, its natural energy will begin to deplete. This will happen every time it is used too.

You can also charge all crystals under the light of a Full Moon, which works really well for pale-coloured crystals in particular. The moon's energy connects to the feminine within us and all things. Our feminine energy is where we find our intuitive, emotional and psychic energies. To charge your crystals under the moon, you can either put them outside overnight or pop them on a windowsill and as with the sun – it doesn't matter if it's cloudy and the moon isn't visible. The energy will still filter down through the clouds.

Activating Your Crystal

Before you use your crystal, you want to set it with your intentions. Hold your crystal in the palm of your hand and imagine beautiful white light flowing out of your hand and surrounding the crystal. This is the universal energy of Qi that flows through all things. You are connecting your crystal to you when you visualise this energy.

You now want to set your intention for your crystal. You could say words such as, 'I set my intentions for this crystal to support me with creating inner peace and calm.'

Your crystal is now ready to use.

Ways to Use Your Crystal

- Place your tumbled crystal in your bra close to your skin for as long as you feel the need. I tend to leave mine there all day.

- Place your crystal in a glass of water or your water bottle and take little sips throughout the day. Be mindful that some crystals are toxic when added to water so make sure you research your crystal to check it is safe to do so first.

- Place your crystal on your body over areas where you have identified that an element is out of balance.

- Hold in the palm of your hand during meditation or visualisation. You can keep it near to you during any of your mindful practices such as journaling.

Earth Crystals

- Black tourmaline
- Smoky quartz
- Obsidian
- Hematite

Air Crystals

- Amethyst
- Clear quartz
- Fluorite
- Celestite

Fire Crystals

- Carnelian
- Red jasper
- Citrine
- Tigers eye

Water Crystals

- Aquamarine
- Blue lace agate
- Lapis lazuli
- Moonston

Soul Questions

What holistic therapy do you feel drawn towards trying?

Just by reading the names of the essential oils, which oil calls to you the strongest?

What crystal name that you have read lingers longer in your mind than any other?

FREEDOM - REFLECTIONS & SUMMARY

Beautiful, freedom-loving Goddess! Within this fifth and final Pillar, you have journeyed to the centre of your heart to understand what freedom means to you. You have identified the lands that call to your soul and have perhaps already begun to plan your sacred pilgrimage! You have let go of any and all regrets that you once carried, understanding that living a life of freedom comes from knowing that every decision that you have ever made was always meant to be made therefore there can be no regrets, only lessons. And finally, you have introduced yourself to a small part of your cosmic blueprint in order to strengthen your connection to the cosmos as well as to the Earth, for they are both *home* within and surrounding you.

Your conscious connection to your sense of freedom is what will keep you unhindered, unrestricted and always with a heart and mind full of possibilities rather than wishes that are always out of reach.

You are exactly where you are meant to be, who you are meant to be and experiencing everything that you were meant to experience. Your mind is now free from the shackles of missed opportunities and regrets, and you are free to say yes to everything that feels right for you because your decision will never be the wrong one.

SOUL QUESTIONS

Have you planned a trip that calls to your soul yet? What places are on your list?

Since reading the chapter on Regret, have you changed your outlook on experiences that you have spent too long regretting? Explain.

How has your most abundant element offered you gifts throughout your life?

What physiological complaints do you have that might link to an elemental imbalance?

YOU HAVE ARRIVED, GODDESS

How do you feel now that your Inner Goddess is sitting firmly atop her throne? We have been on one heck of a ride together, diving deep into the journey of her fall into the shadows and her rise once again into the light.

It would be wishful thinking to hope that your Goddess will remain within the light, for this is not how we are meant to experience life. We are here to experience the duality of our nature and its response and reactions to how our life continues to unfold for us.

Life isn't meant to be one constant, otherwise, we would just experience everything as the same rather than easy or difficult, happy or sad. We wouldn't appreciate the good times without having experienced the bad times. We wouldn't understand what makes us happy without having experienced what makes us unhappy. Life can be a real trial and error, but this is where the growth is. This is where the gifts are that come with living this crazy but beautiful life.

We will find that at some point down the line, we may experience yet again another Dark Night of the Soul, or perhaps we may find old thought patterns have crept back in again, creating negative cyclical patterns within our relationships and our lives. We will naturally become a little less vigilant with our boundaries and may find that we are replaying old stories that keep us stuck once more.

It's ok.

Trust that your Inner Goddess will now kick in and give you a nudge if you have been ignoring her for too long. Your Inner Goddess has now been initiated fully into the Five Pillars of Goddess, therefore they will always be her guide and her reminder if she begins to wander a little too far astray.

Love the life that you have. Honour and celebrate yourself for the journey that you have travelled and the strength that you have gained along the way. Know that you can change the course of your path if you have learnt all that you need from the current one.

Accept that nothing lasts forever and that change is a good thing because it means that you are evolving and growing and that new gifts are about to enter your life.

Let go of regret because all you have is now.

Allow yourself time to process anger and pain and then let them go, replacing them with acceptance and healing.

Dive deep into your past if you need to in order to re-frame your shadows and those of others that you carry. This will also release karma.

Travel to the lands that call to your soul. They will light a fire of creativity, joy and adventure within you.

Nurture your relationship with Mother Earth and with the cosmos in order to find harmony and balance within your health and wellbeing.

And finally, keep your Goddess Philosophy close to your heart, updating it as you evolve and transcend through your life.

My Inner Goddess is sending all of her love to you, my dear friend and fellow Goddess. May your journey continue to be a magical one!

CONNECT WITH ME

Join the Natural Me online community and weave the magic of nature, the moon and the cosmos into your daily wellbeing with a gathering of like-minded Goddesses.

You can find me on my socials over at:

Facebook.com/LisaNaturalMe

Instagram.com/lisa_natural_me

Find out more about our online Natural Me Sisterhood and magical offerings, workbooks and readings over at https://natural-me.teachable.com or www.lisamelbourne.com.

Check out my first book, *Natural Magic for the Modern Goddess* online where all books are sold.

For Amazon UK - https://www.amazon.co.uk/Natural-Magic-Modern-Goddess-Melbourne/dp/1913479749

ACKNOWLEDGEMENTS

This book has been almost three years in the making, and my two little girls have been by my side every step of the way throughout what has been a tough journey and transition for all three of us. My endless love for them and inspiration comes from being so blessed to be their mum. Raising two little Goddesses is truly an epic experience!

Thank you to my close network of Goddesses who have kept me smiling, held me while I have fallen apart, cheered me on when I have wanted to give up and loved me unconditionally when I have been at my lowest as well as my highest. Where would I be without you?

I am so grateful to myself for giving myself the time that I so desperately needed these past three years to accept, acknowledge, heal, love and free my Inner Goddess so that I could find love, peace and happiness once more for who I am at the heart of everything despite what comes my way in life.

And once more, I want to thank you, dear reader and beautiful Goddess, for trusting your intuition and choosing me to walk alongside you on your journey into reclaiming your Inner Goddess. I will forever be in awe of how far the Goddess ripple of intention can travel. I hope to meet you at a future event or retreat coming soon!

Much love to you and so many blessings, for now,

Lisa xx

Printed in Great Britain
by Amazon